Studies in
WRITING & RHETORIC

In 1980, the Conference on College Composition and Communication perceived a need for providing publishing opportunities for monographs that were too long for publication in its journal and too short for the typical scholarly books published by The National Council of Teachers of English. The Studies in Writing and Rhetoric series was conceived, and a Publications Committee established.

Monographs to be considered for publication may be speculative, theoretical, historical, analytical, or empirical studies; or other works contributing to a better understanding of composition and communication, including interdisciplinary studies or studies in related disciplines. The SWR series will exclude textbooks, unrevised dissertations, book-length manuscripts, course syllabi, lesson plans, and collections of previously published material.

Any teacher-writer interested in submitting a work for publication in this series should submit either a prospectus and sample manuscript or a full manuscript to the NCTE Director of Publications, 1111 Kenyon Road, Urbana, IL 61801. Accompanied by sample manuscript, a prospectus should contain a rationale, a definition of readership within the CCCC constituency, comparison with related extant publications, a tentative table of contents, an estimate of length in double-spaced 8½ × 11 sheets, and the date by which full manuscript can be expected. Manuscripts should be in the range of 100 to 170 typed manuscript pages.

The present work serves as a model for future SWR monographs.

Paul O'Dea
NCTE Director of Publications

Evaluating College Writing Programs

Stephen P. Witte and Lester Faigley

WITH A FOREWORD BY LEE ODELL

Published for the Conference on College
Composition and Communication

SOUTHERN ILLINOIS UNIVERSITY PRESS
Carbondale and Edwardsville

Part of the content of this monograph grew out of research supported by a grant from the Fund for the Improvement of Postsecondary Education (Grant G008005896) for which Richard Hendrix serves as Project Officer. The views expressed in the present document do not necessarily reflect those of the funding agency.

Production of works in this series has been partly funded by the Conference on College Composition and Communication of the National Council of Teachers of English.

Printed in the United States of America
Designed by Design for Publishing, Inc., Bob Nance
Production supervised by John DeBacher

Library of Congress Cataloging in Publication Data

Witte, Stephen P. (Stephen Paul), 1943–
  Evaluating college writing programs.

  (Studies in writing and rhetoric)
  Bibliography: p.
  1. English language—Rhetoric—Study and teaching—
Evaluation. I. Faigley, Lester, 1947–   II. Title. III. Series.
PE1404.W57   1983   808'.042'071173   82-19453
ISBN 0-8093-1124-0

To
Jane *and* Linda
and Jeff, Erin, Garth, *and* Ian
who have endured more than we know;
and to
Paul, Roger, Anna, Keith, David,
Mary, *and* Tom
who have given more than they know.

Contents

Tables

Foreword

Lee Odell

What do we need to find out when we evaluate a writing program? How do we determine whether a program is all that it should be? On the face of it, the answer seems simple enough. We need to know whether student writing is improving, whether students at the end of a course (or series of courses) are writing better than they were at the beginning. To determine whether student writing has improved, what we need to do is compare writing students did early in the program with writing they did later in the program.

This sort of comparison does provide information of a sort that, at one time might have seemed quite adequate. However, as we read *Evaluating College Writing Programs*, it becomes clear that we may no longer assume that evaluating student writing is the same thing as evaluating a composition program. As Witte and Faigley point out, a writing program is much more than a collection of student papers. It is a complex set of interrelated activities that exist in an even more complex set of scholarly, institutional, and interpersonal contexts. To evaluate a writing program, we must answer a number of questions, only one of which pertains to the improvement of student writing.

Do we, in fact, have a writing program? Many composition programs are staffed by a wide range of faculty—part-time instructors, graduate students, full-time faculty whose principal scholarly interest may or may not be composition. Consequently, we need to ask: "Do these faculty share any common assumptions concerning the teaching of composition? Are those assumptions reflected in their assignments, evaluative procedures, teaching procedures, and course content?

If we do have a writing program, how stable will it prove over time? What are the forces—e.g., administrative decisions, changes in student population—that are likely to influence faculty morale and/or performance?

Is the program likely to have any long-term influence on students' writing? Do students leave the program with increased confidence in their ability? Do they find any connection between the writing they did for their composition course and the writing they do for other courses? Indeed, do they actually write for other courses or is the composition program some sort of oasis/anomaly?

This list of questions is neither exhaustive nor arbitrary. As Witte and Faigley make clear, we are just beginning to understand the kinds of issues writing program evaluators must consider. To identify these issues, Witte and Faigley review four major evaluation studies, asking about each a series of questions that apply to every aspect of theory, pedagogy, and research: What do we presently know? What assumptions are we making and how do those assumptions limit our knowledge? Are those limitations necessary or desirable? What do we still need to know?

By asking such basic questions as these, Witte and Faigley will not make life any easier for program evaluators. Witte and Faigley make it clear that we cannot evade certain questions if we want to claim we have evaluated a writing program. Yet even as they help us see new questions, they also help us understand the conceptual framework that makes these questions important and that promises to enable us to answer these questions.

Perhaps more important, Witte and Faigley's work lets the Publication Committee of Studies in Writing and Rhetoric articulate one of our main concerns. At present, it could easily be argued that many composition programs do not represent a discipline but rather are an *ad hoc* response to the current literacy crisis. To establish beyond question the authenticity of composition as a discipline, we must have some agreement about theory, methodology, and the kinds of questions that are worth asking. We hope that the Witte and Faigley text—and, indeed, all the titles in this series—will help us work toward that agreement and, ultimately, toward the establishment of composition as a discipline.

Troy, New York
January 1983

Acknowledgments

Our work on *Evaluating College Writing Programs* commenced at about the same time as we—together with colleagues Jim Kinneavy and John Daly—began drafting a grant proposal for the Fund for the Improvement of Postsecondary Education. Although this monograph and the FIPSE proposal were conceived as two separate projects, they quickly merged when in the fall of 1980 we were awarded a three-year grant from FIPSE to develop materials and procedures for evaluating college writing programs.

From the outset of the FIPSE project, our two fellow investigators—Jim Kinneavy and John Daly—served, at the very least, as sounding boards for many of the ideas about writing program evaluation which we set out in the following pages. Also from the beginning of the FIPSE project, Richard Hendrix, our Project Officer, continually challenged—sometimes in not so subtle ways—us to think through more carefully many of the ideas which eventually were to become a part of the present work. *Evaluating College Writing Programs* has also benefited enormously from the many hours we have spent discussing writing program evaluation with our FIPSE consultants—Linda Flower (Carnegie Mellon University), Sarah Freedman (University of California, Berkeley), Richard Larson (Herbert Lehman College), Richard Lloyd-Jones (University of Iowa), and Ellen Nold (Stanford University). We are particularly grateful to Sarah Freedman and Richard Larson who read and commented on the monograph in draft. Most importantly, *Evaluating College Writing Programs* has in a very real way grown out of our work with the graduate students who have labored with us on the FIPSE project—Roger Cherry, David Jolliffe, Paul Meyer, Tom Miller, Anna Skinner, Mary Trachsel, and Keith Walters. To these graduate students, we owe much more than this simple note of gratitude. No one could ask for a better group of colleagues with whom to work.

We would also like to express our thanks to Paul O'Dea, NCTE Director of Publications, and the CCCC Committee on Research for the support they have given to the writing of the present monograph. We are particularly grateful to Lee Odell (Rensselaer Polytechnic Institute) for his sage and thorough commentaries on two earlier versions.

Austin, Texas
January 1983

Evaluating College Writing Programs

1

The State of the Art of Evaluating Writing Programs

I. 1. *The Need for Evaluation*

"OCTOBER," MARK TWAIN IS REPORTED TO HAVE SAID, "IS ONE of the peculiarly dangerous months to speculate in stocks. Others are July, January, September, April, November, May, March, June, December, August and February." The same could be said about the evaluation of college writing programs. Nevertheless, whether by choice or circumstance, most composition specialists eventually participate in an evaluation of a writing program, gathering and interpreting pieces of information that will contribute to decisions about the program or particular courses in it. From the conception of an evaluation, from the planning stage to the final report, the evaluator of college writing programs must confront a variety of difficult questions. Among these questions are the following: What purposes will the evaluation serve? Should the person(s) charged with evaluating a writing course or program be directly associated with it? What will be the basis or bases of judgments about the program? Will teachers' testimonials be accepted as evidence of the program's effectiveness? How will the different evaluation data be relied upon in judgments about the program? Will student performance or achievement be considered the most important source of evaluation data? If measures of student performance are deemed acceptable as sources of evaluation data, how will those measures be administered? Will the methods and the procedures of the evaluation affect the normal pattern of learning? Should the evaluator know the expected outcomes of the program in advance of the evaluation? Are quantitative or qualitative methods to be used, or are both to be used? Which will be weighted most heavily? Are attitudinal and affective changes in students as well as cognitive ones to be measured? Are the instruments for doing so valid and reliable? Are sufficient funds going to be made available to carry out the evaluation?

Although evaluations of writing programs are carried out each year in many colleges and universities across the country, the literature on composition research is with but few exceptions silent on how to answer questions such as the ones we have posed. This is not to say that no body of scholarship addresses evaluation. To the contrary, even a hastily conducted library search will turn up numerous books and articles addressing the philosophical[1] and practical[2] issues of evaluation. Only recently, however, have composition specialists begun to recognize the importance and the complexity of evaluating an entire writing program, to realize that evaluating a college writing program involves much more than assessing the written products of students at the beginning and the ending of a term. Major efforts toward improving evaluation, however, are being made by Richard Larson's Conference on College Composition and Communication Committee on Teaching and Its Evaluation in Composition,[3] the Bay Area Writing Project,[4] and the Writing Program Assessment Project at The University of Texas at Austin.[5] Groups such as these have begun to explore some of the many crucial questions associated with the evaluation of college writing programs. Yet the literature on composition research gives would-be evaluators very little to guide them through the maze of philosophical, theoretical, and methodological problems.

Evaluation research is usually lumped together with pedagogical research under the more general rubric of applied research. Unlike basic research, where the emphasis is on the generation of new knowledge for its own sake, applied research strives to put knowledge to use in practical situations. In part because of its concern for the pragmatic, pedagogical research in general and evaluation research in particular are sometimes viewed as poor second cousins to the important basic research in most disciplines. Research in writing is no exception. Some researchers have called for what amounts to a moratorium on applied research until more basic questions about writing have been explored.[6]

In spite of its lack of prestige, applied research in writing is likely to continue. Pedagogical research takes as its goal the development and testing of effective composition curricula and instructional methods, and evaluation research takes as its goal the justification of curricula and instruction. In a discipline committed to the teaching of writing, certainly both goals are important. Yet pedagogical and evaluation research are, and will continue to be, important for two other reasons: (1) they can identify significant questions for basic research, and (2) they can provide some measure of accountability for a profession becoming increasingly more accountable to agencies beyond its control.

At the time of the publication of Braddock, Lloyd-Jones, and Schoer's *Research in Written Composition* in 1963,[7] research in writing was almost exclusively concerned with pedagogy, with how best to teach students to write. In the nearly two decades which have followed, composition research has diversified considerably, with a great body of basic research appearing on discourse theory, composing, and writing development. Often overlooked, however, is how much of this basic research has been inspired by pedagogical research. The most obvious example of how pedagogical research can influence basic research in composition is the work of Rohman and Wlecke in the early 1960s.[8] Their study was designed and executed as a pedagogical experiment in which the writing of two treatment groups was compared in order to evaluate one pedagogical treatment against the other. Ironically, the Rohman and Wlecke study opened up the composing process as an area of investigation. The influence of their study on basic research in writing has been considerable, even though their three-stage linear model of composing—prewriting, writing, and rewriting—has been dismissed. More recently, pedagogical studies of the effects of sentence combining have led to speculations about the cognitive processes associated with writing development and have focused more attention on units of discourse above the sentence level.[9]

Apart from comparing the effectiveness of instructional methods and curricula and generating basic research questions, the most obvious reason for continuing evaluation research is that public institutions in a democracy are accountable to the public. Accountability of writing programs has become a much more prominent issue in the aftermath of the "literacy crisis" of the 1970s. Based on the results of several national surveys of language abilities—such as those conducted under the auspices of the National Assessment of

Educational Progress (NAEP)[10]—many articles in the popular press and many broadcasts and telecasts during the past decade reported that writing abilities are declining at all educational levels. Although these articles have proffered a number of reasons for the decline, most echo the conclusion of the widely quoted *Newsweek* article, "Why Johnny Can't Write": "the U.S. educational system is spawning a generation of semiliterates."[11]

In response to the "literacy crisis," many colleges and universities have inserted new requirements into their curricula and developed new programs for teaching writing;[12] and private and federal agencies have supported several recent attempts to make college writing instruction more effective. Whether these innovations are indeed improving the writing abilities of college students and whether they are in fact better than older methods remains very much in doubt, primarily because neither evaluation theory nor practice has adequately accommodated the discipline-specific needs of writing programs and courses. Not to advance discipline-specific theories and practices of evaluation may have the effect of stripping the profession of the one means it has for demonstrating the usefulness of its own solutions to the so-called literacy crisis. If we as composition teachers and researchers do not develop our own models for evaluating our writing programs, others will surely do it for us.

The purpose of the present monograph is to set out a theoretical framework for evaluating college writing programs. We do not propose solutions to the many problems associated with evaluation. Rather, we intend this framework to be used to generate the kinds of questions that will lead to comprehensive evaluations. We are intentionally pluralistic and eclectic, drawing on many sources in constructing this framework. To the extent that our monograph will help persons interested in evaluation to understand better the complex and dynamic nature of college writing programs, our efforts will be worthwhile.

I. 2. *Two Dominant Approaches to Writing Program Evaluation*

It is curious that so little has been written on the theory of writing program evaluation. A vast literature on evaluation exists for other disciplines, and issues concerning evaluation date back as far as college writing courses themselves. Even before the turn of the century, inferences about the effectiveness of instruction were made on the basis of writing samples.[13] And today, many judgments are made about the effectiveness of writing programs on the basis of limited evidence, such as the year-to-year scores on exit examinations from writing courses. Even though many writing program directors believe that such measures do not adequately reflect the complex mission of writing programs, their frustration has brought few efforts to amend the situation.

If there is no developed body of theory for writing program evaluation, writing programs are nevertheless evaluated with some frequency using one of two approaches. The first and most common approach is the *expert-opinion approach.* The usual procedure in this approach is for an "expert" to visit a writing program and then judge its merits. The evaluation depends heavily on the expert's impressions and knowledge, thus making the evaluator central in the evaluation of the program. This approach is an extension of *nonprogrammatic* evaluations routinely conducted in colleges and universities. In such nonprogrammatic evaluations, teachers of writing are called upon to evaluate students, colleagues, courses, textbooks, curricula, departments, and administrators.

In spite of its widespread use, we refrain from calling the expert-opinion approach a model for evaluation. Even though the expert-opinion approach seems to provide the basis of the Council for Writing Program Administrators' forays into evaluation, we have been able to find very few accessible documents describing either instances or rationales for this approach. In one such document, the WPA Board of Consultant Evaluators lists a series of questions capable of generating descriptions of many components of writing programs. However, the WPA Board never indicates how the resultant descriptions should figure in program evaluations. The WPA Board apparently sees no distinction between description and evaluation: while it offers its set of questions as "a tool that WPAs and their colleagues may find useful in reviewing their programs' goals, needs, and procedures," it provides no guidance for arriving at evaluative judgments.[14]

In practice, the expert-opinion approach varies a great deal from evaluator to evaluator, from site to site. In some locations evaluators collect descriptions—in the form of course descriptions and syllabi —of the program being evaluated; in others they do not. In some locations evaluators talk to teachers and students; in others they do not. In some locations evaluators visit classes; in others they do not. In some locations evaluators examine student papers; in others they do not. The only common denominator seems to be the presence of an "expert," the definition of which is as obscure as the approach itself.

If we cannot construct a model for the expert-opinion approach, we can identify some of its underlying assumptions. First, as Gardner and House both urge,[15] the principal assumption is that the best evaluator is an expert on the thing or activity being evaluated. This assumption, however valid it may appear on the surface, is open to question. In the evaluation of writing programs, a good deal hangs on one's identification of "expert." Is an expert evaluator of a writing program someone who is acknowledged as an effective teacher of writing? Is an expert someone who has successfully directed a writing program in another setting? Is an expert someone who is a member of this or that professional group? Is an expert someone who has written textbooks for college writing classes? Is an expert someone who understands and contributes regularly to the development of new knowledge in the field? Is an expert someone who espouses a particular theory of writing, or curriculum, or instruction? The inherent weakness of this underlying assumption is that very few experts tend to be knowledgeable in all areas of writing programs.

A second assumption, namely, that the criteria upon which judgments are made are appropriate, derives from the first assumption. This second assumption runs contrary to the nature of expertise since expert judgments are likely to be colored by the particular area of expertise. Someone who is an expert in organizational theory may be able to make valid judgments about the effectiveness of the administrative structure of the writing program but be incapable of making valid judgments about the appropriateness of a specific curricular component. Similarly, a textbook writer may be a responsible judge of the organization and presentation of text materials but not have the expertise required to make judgments about the suitability of the text materials to the institution's goals. In all possible approaches to writing program evaluation, but especially in the expert-opinion approach, Kenneth Burke's reminder that a way of seeing is also a way of not seeing seems apropos.

A third assumption of the expert-opinion approach emanates from the first two: that the expert or experts selected to evaluate the program are capable of processing all of the relevant evaluation data in order to make judgments based on those data. There is considerable evidence that experts who share the same background knowledge combine data in different ways to arrive at sometimes disparate judgments.[16] In addition, expert-opinion evaluations rarely acknowledge principles of sample selections or generalizability when considering evidence, nor do they make use of qualitative methods of evaluations because "experts" in writing seldom are trained in these areas.

As a consequence of these assumptions, the expert-opinion approach to writing program evaluation is largely atheoretical, making any evaluation model impossible to extrapolate. In some instances, experts have perhaps given sound evaluations of writing programs. But experts have also been used to make programs appear better than they are or to delay unfavorable administrative decisions. Since the results of expert-opinion evaluations usually are not published or presented at professional meetings, there have been no advances in this approach over the years. All is dependent upon the knowledge, biases, commitment, and sensitivity of the evaluator.

The second dominant approach—a quantitative one which typically uses pretest-posttest designs—also lacks an articulated theoretical basis. The quantitative approach, however, differs significantly from the expert-opinion approach in several ways. The evaluator is not at the center of the evaluation. Instead of relying on subjective impressions, an evaluator seeks objectivity in quantitative measures which can be used across evaluation settings. Quantitative evaluations are frequently published, allowing other researchers to examine their assumptions, methodologies, and results. Researchers have attempted to learn from other researchers in order to refine their research designs and procedures.

While there is no articulated model for conducting quantitative evaluations of writing programs, we believe such a model exists and has informed some major pretest-posttest studies of writing programs during the past two decades. In the next chapter, we extrapolate that model.

2

The Quantitative Model of Writing Program Evaluation

IN CHAPTER 1 WE ARGUED THAT THERE HAVE BEEN TWO DOMInant approaches to writing program evaluation—the expert-opinion approach, which is an *ad hoc* response to the need for evaluation, and the pretest-posttest approach, which is based on an unarticulated model for writing program evaluation. In this chapter, we will examine that unarticulated model by reviewing four major pretest-posttest evaluation studies: the University of Northern Iowa study, the University of California San Diego study, the Miami University study, and the University of Texas study. We might have chosen other studies as well, but these four serve to raise the most important issues evaluators must face. The four studies focus in different ways on two related questions: Does college writing instruction positively affect the development of writing abilities? and Is one type of composition instruction more effective than another? Together these studies point to the need to accommodate the large number of curricular, instructional, and contextual variables of college writing programs in an evaluation design.

II. 1. *The University of Northern Iowa Study*

Most evaluations of college writing instruction have addressed the issue of whether one kind of writing instruction is more effective than another. One exception is the study conducted at the University of Northern Iowa by Ross M. Jewell, John Cowley, and Gordon

Rhum.[1] The Northern Iowa study sought an answer to the broader
question, Does any kind of college writing instruction make a difference in the writing abilities of college students? We chose to examine this study because it illustrates two problems that frequently
appear in evaluations of writing programs and courses: (1) the failure to understand and accommodate differences between composition courses, and (2) the failure to recognize and control differences
between noncomposition courses of study.

II. 1. 1. The Design and Results of the Northern Iowa Study
   The Northern Iowa study paired 2,080 freshmen enrolled at five
different universities in the fall of 1964. The paired students were
matched on the basis of sex, ACT or SAT score, a theme score, and a
score indicative of combined performance on the Cooperative English Tests: English Expression (COOP) and the College Entrance
Examination Board English Composition Test (CEEB). One member of the 1,040 pairs took courses in writing and in other academic
subjects while the other member took courses in other subjects only.
   Jewell, Cowley, and Rhum report that three tests—the COOP,
the CEEB, and a theme—were administered to the students in the
study at four different times, once near the beginning of their college careers and once at the end of the first, second, and fourth semesters of study. The COOP and the CEEB, which are both objective tests, were scored according to the publishers' guidelines; and
the themes were rated by Educational Testing Service personnel
using the procedures then employed by ETS.[2] The analyses performed on the Northern Iowa data generally indicated that at the
end of the first two semesters, the students who were enrolled in
composition performed better than their paired counterparts who
were not. However, by the end of the fourth semester, students
who had received no formal instruction in college-level writing performed as well as those students who had received writing instruction as freshmen. Jewell and his colleagues thus concluded that
freshman composition teaches writing skills that develop naturally,
but at some later point in the student's academic career.

II. 1. 2. A Critique of the Northern Iowa Study
   The Northern Iowa study has suggested to many that teaching
courses in freshman writing is pointless, a conclusion which Jewell,

Cowley, and Rhum did not themselves draw. Yet the study does suggest that courses in freshman composition may be of limited value. But even that tentative conclusion may be questioned, given the design of the study and some of the assumptions which underlie the design.

Although impressively complex and ambitious, the Northern Iowa study has a number of flaws in its design. These flaws resulted primarily from two assumptions the Northern Iowa investigators made prior to collecting the data on which their analyses were based. Both assumptions concerned the nature of the writing programs at the five participating universities. First, the investigators failed to acknowledge in their research design differences among the five programs, even though their descriptions (see pp. 23–24) of the five composition programs indicate that considerable variation among the programs existed, both in terms of "content" (their term) and in terms of the amount and kinds of writing the students did. Indeed, the "composition program" at one participating university—The University of Iowa—was quite unlike any of the other programs. Second, the investigators did not attend to differences in instructional methods used in the various programs or by individual teachers within a particular composition program. These two assumptions led the Northern Iowa investigators to ignore differences in curriculum, student populations, program and course goals or objectives, and instructional methods.

The Northern Iowa evaluation also assumed that all noncomposition instruction which either group of students received was undifferentiated, both within and across the five institutions. That is to say, the investigators assumed that taking a course of study in chemistry affects the development of writing abilities no differently than taking a course of study in art history or literature. However, an alternative assumption—that different courses of study had different effects on students' writing abilities—is perhaps the more plausible one. For example, students enrolled in an engineering degree program probably did considerably less reading and less writing during their first two academic years than did students enrolled in a program leading to a degree in history. Jewell, Cowley, and Rhum remained silent about three important matters embedded in their second assumption: the nature of the degree programs in which the students were enrolled, how these degree programs may have differed in promoting language skills, and the distribution of individual subjects and of paired subjects in the different courses of study within and across the five universities.

The investigators' failure to explore these assumptions and their failure to control the variables these assumptions ignore make the results of their comparisons difficult to interpret. If the 1,040 matched pairs formed at the beginning of the study had remained in the study for the full two years, these assumptions would be less problematic than they are, and the influence of particular instructional programs, whether in composition or in other disciplines, on the results might have been less. By the end of the first semester, however, the 1,040 pairs were reduced through attrition to 597 pairs; by the end of the second semester, to 365 pairs; and by the end of the fourth semester, to 122 pairs, slightly more than 10 percent of the original sample. If the five composition programs had been identical in all respects (but they were not) and if the noncomposition courses of study had been identical (but they probably were not) for the remaining 122 pairs, we could place more confidence in the results of the study. However, the Northern Iowa investigators did not report the distribution of the 122 pairs either within composition programs or within noncomposition courses of study in any of the five universities.

The problems which result from ignoring such variables are many. For example, if a substantial number of the 122 students enrolled in freshman composition courses were enrolled in a particular composition program, any differences between the two groups' performances at the end of the fourth semester might be attributed to the ineffectiveness of one particular composition program among the five used, rather than to the ineffectiveness of freshman composition in general. Attention to curricular, instructional, and contextual variables is mandatory in well-designed evaluation research.

The two assumptions we have addressed—that all composition courses are equivalent and that all noncomposition courses are equivalent—illustrate the need for careful attention to complex sets of interacting variables, whether they be contextual, curricular, or instructional in nature. Although we have criticized the design of the Northern Iowa study, we have not condemned the study itself, for the investigators present virtually all of their findings cautiously. The Northern Iowa study is one of the most ambitious and most complex evaluation studies of freshman composition ever attempted. In fact, its complexity is one reason the study was selected for review here. Those who undertake such complex endeavors deserve nothing but our respect, for the difficulties they encounter are many.

II. 2. *The University of California San Diego Study*

While the Northern Iowa study sought to determine whether any kind of writing program increases writing ability, most evaluation studies have been primarily concerned with finding answers to the second question we posed earlier: Is one method of teaching freshman composition more effective than another? Several studies have addressed the question directly, but one study addressed it indirectly. That study is the one recently completed under the direction of Donald Wesling at the University of California San Diego.[3] The differences between the "programs" evaluated in the San Diego study are very much like the differences between "equivalent" courses within the same program. We selected the San Diego study for review here because (1) unlike the Northern Iowa study, it attempted to accommodate differences in the way writing is taught, (2) it relied on more than one measure of writing course or program effectiveness, (3) it illustrates some of the difficulties associated with infering course or program effectiveness from writing samples, and (4) it illustrates the relative nature of writing program evaluation.

II. 2. 1. The Design and Results of the San Diego Study

The subjects used in the San Diego study were 175 freshmen unevenly distributed across the four colleges within the University. Each of the four groups—which ranged in size from 35 to 50 students—produced three essays which were submitted to holistic evaluation on a nine-point scale by two independent raters, with a third rater used to reconcile large differences between the scores assigned by the first two raters. Each of the four groups received instruction in writing, but that instruction differed considerably across groups. For example, while two of the colleges' composition programs were tied to the contents of other disciplines, the other two were not. One of the programs tied to another content required students to write on social issues, deriving topics from a reader, while the other required its students to write on topics from the humanities. All four groups of students were reported to have significantly increased their average holistic scores from the first to the second essay and from the first to the third essay.

Some of the students also took the English Achievement Test (EAT) at two different times, once prior to admission and once after completing a course in college writing. This pretest-posttest use of the EAT was adopted in order to determine whether writing instruction in the four colleges "led to improvement in the editing component of writing" (p. 21). In addition, the EAT was administered to a group of students who had not been exposed to writing instruction in any of the four colleges. Analyses of the EAT results indicated that none of the five groups—the four groups drawn from the four colleges nor the "control" group—realized statistically significant gains on the EAT.

In addition to the use of three essays as measures of the students' writing abilities and the two administrations of the EAT as measures of "editing skills," the San Diego study employed a number of other evaluative tools. For example, James Moffett[4] served as an "outside" evaluator who visited classes, talked with teachers and administrators, and solicited reactions to the four programs from students. The investigators also collected reactions from students to the composition programs in which they were enrolled. For this purpose, the investigators used a 37-item course and professor evaluation questionnaire, a locally designed Likert-type instrument which apparently had been used at San Diego for several years. In addition, 33 students were interviewed by persons involved in the study in an attempt to arrive at some "confirmation of impressions" generated from other sources of data (p. 45).

II. 2. 2. Critique of the San Diego Study

The report of the San Diego evaluation concludes that in general the four undergraduate colleges at UC San Diego did equally effective jobs in improving students' writing.

The study is not, however, free of problems in research design and methodology, some of which are noted by the investigators.[5] These problems in design and methodology need to be placed in perspective, since the San Diego evaluation was an evaluation quite different from the Northern Iowa study. Whereas the Northern Iowa evaluation sought, in effect, to determine the relative efficacy of two different treatments—one involving composition instruction and one not—the purpose of the San Diego study was "to try to evaluate programmatic strengths and weaknesses of each college program in context rather than in competition" (p. 34). Thus overt comparisons of the writing programs of the four colleges were presumably beyond the scope of the San Diego evaluation; however, Wesling and his colleagues structured the report and evaluated the writing samples in such a way that implicit, if not explicit, comparisons across the four colleges were made throughout.

The features of the San Diego study which make comparisons across the four programs difficult can be illustrated very easily. If, for example, the investigators had been serious about evaluating each of the four programs "in context rather than in competition," then it would have made more sense to write a separate report for each program. Instead, the investigators chose to write a single report in which, among other things, they put in the same table the results for the four colleges and employ such expressions as "cross-college comparison," "Warren, unlike the other colleges," and "highest in Third College." Throughout the report, the reader is invited to make the very comparisons the investigators say they intended to avoid.

These comparisons were, in fact, unavoidable, given the procedures used for conducting the holistic evaluations. The investigators recognized that the four college writing programs differed in important ways from one another. One of the ways in which they differed was in the kinds of writing the students in the various colleges were asked to do, a matter documented by the investigators themselves. Indeed, the researchers included the following sentence in their report: "Among the variables we could not control for: discourse mode, the amount of time elapsed between essays, the number of hours of instruction, different forms of instruction, differing amounts of collateral reading, differing ways of generating topics for writing" (pp. 34–35). One might be inclined to think that the lack of control over these variables would be inconsequential in an evaluation whose purpose was not to compare four composition programs but rather to evaluate each program in its own context. However, the essays—which were written on different topics, in different modes, and at different times by the four groups—were pooled for the holistic evaluations. Thus the raters knew the topic of an essay if it was "indicated . . . by the title" (if there was one) or "by whatever the reader . . . [could] infer from the thrust of the given piece of writing" (p. 28).

In holistic scoring, judgments of writing quality are always relative. Raters give a particular score to a particular paper in relation to the scores assigned to the other papers in the set. A holistic training session might be defined as the process by which experienced raters of student writing are forced through group pressure to abandon their own ideas of writing quality and to adopt others which are relative to the rating group's view of writing quality, relative to the set of essays being rated, and relative to the need to distribute essays across all scoring categories. Whenever ratings—whether holistic or otherwise—are made relative to all the papers in the set, all ratings are based on explicit and implicit comparisons among the papers in the set.

With the papers from the four colleges pooled, the raters in the San Diego study had no choice but to compare the writing of students in one college with the writing of students in other colleges to determine the merit of one essay in relation to all other essays in the set regardless of the topic on which the essays were written, the rhetorical purpose for which they were written, and the modes in which they were written. In short, the procedures employed mandated comparing essays across colleges. These very comparisons, however, were the ones the investigators indicated could not be made because the four writing programs were fundamentally different. Thus while the San Diego investigators sought to avoid one of the problems we identified in the Northern Iowa study, they did not do so.

Although we have been criticial of certain features of the San Diego evaluation study, we believe that Wesling and his colleagues are to be commended for recognizing that use of a single source of data will not result in a good writing program evaluation. Because of this recognition, the San Diego investigators collected and analyzed different kinds of data from a number of different sources—objective measures of writing ability, writing samples, measures of student attitudes towards courses and instructors, personal observations and interviews by an "outside" expert, and in-depth interviews of students. No single set of data provided the basis for the positive evaluation accorded the four writing programs; rather, the investigators used all available data as the basis for their evaluation of the four programs.

Because no generally acceptable procedures and materials for evaluating writing programs have been developed, we have limited our criticism of the San Diego study to aspects of the holistic evaluation of the student papers. Although not all of the issues of reliability and validity have been addressed, procedures for evaluating student texts holistically have been established and the nature of such evaluation has been defined,[6] thus justifying our criticism. Our criticism of the particular method of rating the San Diego papers holistically raises some important questions about the validity of that procedure, for a method can be valid for a particular purpose only if it is consistent with that purpose. The lesson to be learned from the San Diego study is that writing program evaluators must develop and use research procedures consistent with the purpose of the evaluation.

II. 3. *The Miami University Study*

Some studies have attempted to avoid the problem illustrated by the San Diego study by comparing different approaches to teaching college writing. These studies try to control, through both research designs and statistical procedures, the major curricular and instructional variables. However, these variables are very difficult to control, as illustrated by the Miami University sentence-combining study conducted by Andrew Kerek, Donald Daiker, and Max Morenberg. The purpose of the Miami study was to determine the effectiveness of a "sentence-combining curriculum" in comparison to a "traditional" composition course.[7] The Miami study was selected for review here because it (1) illustrates the difficulties associated with the failure to separate curricular and instructional variables involved in comparative evaluations of writing courses, (2) illustrates the problems of defining both curricula and instruction in writing, and (3) illustrates the necessity of controlling instructional and curricular variables through carefully conceived research designs.

II. 3. 1. The Design and Results of the Miami Study

In the Miami study, 290 beginning college freshmen were used to form two groups consisting of six classes each. One group was called a "control" group and the other was called an "experimental" group, even though both groups underwent writing instruction of some kind.[8] The "experimental" group, consisting of 151 subjects, was exposed to what the Miami investigators called "an exclusive sentence-combining curriculum,"[9] while the other, consisting of 139 subjects, was exposed to "traditional"[10] instruction in writing. Pretest and posttest essays were collected from all students. These essays were written on an informative or expository topic that allowed students to draw narrative and descriptive details from personal experience. These essays were collected from each group at the beginning and ending of a semester of study. In addition, the investigators also collected pre- and posttest reading scores. When the reading scores were compared, neither group was found to have improved in reading skills more than the other. However, when the holistic and analytic scores assigned to the writing samples were compared, the investigators found that the "experimental" group had realized significantly larger gains in writing quality than had the "control" group. So too with comparisons of the writing samples along certain dimensions of syntactic fluency.[11]

A follow-up study was also conducted 28 months after the original data had been collected. Of the original 290 students, 140 participated in the follow-up, 65 from the "control" group and 75 from the "experimental" group. The follow-up was conducted in order "to investigate the long-range effects of intensive sentence-combining practice on the writing ability of college students" (p. 1130). The 140 students in the follow-up study were volunteers who were paid to write one essay on the same topic they had written for the posttest essay in the original study. These 140 new essays were pooled with those essays originally written as posttest essays by the same students. This set of 280 essays was then rated holistically and analytically by ETS raters who were reported not to have known the source of the essays they were asked to rate. Analyses of the follow-up ratings revealed that "on both the holistic and the analytic ratings, the control-experimental differences were statistically not significant" (p. 1133), that the "sentence-combining students were no longer superior to the control students in writing quality" (p. 1134).

The Miami investigators initially speculated that the qualitative increases on the experimental students' posttest essays were strongly linked to the quantitative gains in Hunt's syntactic indices, since the group taught by sentence combining increased significantly in both holistic scores and syntactic measures while the traditionally taught group did not.[12] Other researchers who examined the relationship between syntactic maturity and judgments of quality, however, found Hunt's indices to be minimumly valuable for explaining variance in holistic sources.[13] When the Miami investigators analyzed the amount of the variance in holistic ratings of experimental posttests which could be accounted for by Hunt's indices, they found that the syntactic factors together "predicted not quite 4% of the . . . variance" (p. 1126). Thus the raters were not influenced to any great degree by the increased complexity in the sentence combiners' posttest essays.

II. 3. 2. Critique of the Miami Study

The Miami investigators encountered several problems in defining the curricular and instructional variables in their study, a fact which finds illustration in the differing accounts of the study. These problems stem from the investigators' failure to determine prior to the study itself whether they were to examine a curriculum, and instructional method, or both. The 1980 and most recent version of the Miami study offers *post hoc* explanations of why sentence combining worked and attempts to answer some of the criticisms and questions raised about the study as originally reported.[14] For example, Mellon and Kinneavy pointed out that the whole-discourse exercises used in the Miami study differed substantially from the sentence-combining exercises used by Mellon and O'Hare in earlier studies. The Miami investigators did not address this issue in their 1978 reports; but in the 1980 report, they write that the "experimental students were exposed to *rhetorically based* [italics theirs] sentence combining," that "the sentence-combining method used in the experimental sections was deliberately and unabashedly rhetorical in character" (p. 1099). Elsewhere in the report, the investigators say that "the term 'sentence combining' is not a wholly accurate description of the classroom procedures used in the experimental sections: sentence-combining practice obviously went far beyond isolated, sentence-level grammatical transformations" (p.

1100). Clearly, the Miami investigators faced a difficult problem in definition, a problem which turned on not only the activity of combining "kernel" sentences into longer ones and the kinds of sentence-combining exercises used but also the classroom procedures the teachers of the experimental classes used to lead their students to an understanding of the rhetorical principles they wished to emphasize. Obviously, the Miami investigators had expanded the notion of sentence combining to include the notion of discourse combining and discourse generation as well.

The Miami investigators' expansion of the notion of sentence combining as inherited from Mellon[15] and O'Hare[16] was nothing short of inspired. Yet because this expansion was not carefully defined prior to the study itself, it created a serious design problem for the investigators, as reflected in their inability to distinguish between sentence combining as a "teaching method" (p. 1116) and sentence combining as a curriculum: "The idea of an exclusive sentence-combining curriculum had not been tested before" (p. 1101).

If we understand *curriculum* in its usual sense of "content" and if we understand *teaching method* or *instructional method* in its usual sense of the means and ways used to teach curriculum, then the major problem in the Miami study becomes obvious. Sentence combining is not a writing curriculum; rather it is an instructional method.

The instructional method of combining short sentences into one or more sentences contains no inherent assumptions about the resulting sentences. That is to say, as originally conceived, sentence combining in and of itself did not teach a content, did not address rhetorical concerns; it taught students how to combine sentences independently of rhetorical situations. Mellon, for example, used sentence combining to accelerate naturally occurring syntactic development, not to teach the use of rhetorical principles. But the Miami study employed sentence combining in a very different way, and for an additional reason. In the following quotation, which illustrates the instructional materials and methods growing out of the Miami study, the Miami investigators use sentence combining to teach rhetorical principles. Here they discuss three students' solutions to a sentence-combining problem: "All three student writers apparently realize that repeating key terms or sentence elements, especially at the conclusion of an essay, is an effective means of emphasis. But all have problems making repetition work. In the first version, the fragment is more disruptive than emphatic."[17] This adaptation of sentence combining to teach rhetorical principles contained in traditional writing curricula is an important innovation, one which makes sentence combining an instructional method appropriate for college writing classes. But the rhetorical principles themselves are matters of curriculum, not the method or methods used to teach it.[18] In short, the Miami investigators were unable to decide whether they were testing for the relative effectiveness of a curriculum or an instructional method or both. Consequently, they failed to control some important variables, both instructional and curricular, in their study.

Among the variables left uncontrolled in the Miami study were the amount of writing the students in the two groups did, the amount of collateral reading they did, the kinds of writing they did, the rhetorical principles they were taught, the textbooks they used, the amount and kinds of homework assignments they did, and the apparently diverse set of instructional methods used in the two classes.[19] These are essentially some of the same variables which were left uncontrolled in the Northern Iowa study and in the San Diego study. With this many variables left uncontrolled, it is—contrary to the claims of the Miami investigators—impossible to tell whether the "experimental" classes promoted greater growth in syntactic fluency and writing quality or whether the "control" classes inhibited such growth. If one adopts the position of the Miami investigators that the "experimental" classes promoted such growth, determining which instructional or curricular variable(s) caused the growth is similarly impossible.

The investigators explain their failure to control one of these variables in the following way:

> The experimental students did more out-of-class writing than their control counterparts. Since all sentence-combining exercises require students to write, experimental students spent much of their homework time writing, just as control students spent much of their time reading. After all, homework assignments that require writing are as integral to a sentence-combining program as those that require reading are to a program with an essay reader and a standard rhetoric. It follows that equalizing the total amount of writing by the control and experimental students would have meant changing the fundamental nature of at least one of the

two curriculums. But such control may have been as unnecessary as it was undesirable, because research suggests that neither the amount nor the frequency of writing in itself improves writing quality. (p. 1102)

While it is true that some research—research on high school writers—suggests that "neither the amount nor the frequency of writing in itself improves writing quality," the amount and the frequency of "writing in itself" is not what is at issue in the Miami study. What is at issue is the variability in the amount and frequency of writing in conjunction with the variability in instructional methods, kinds of writing, amount and frequency of reading, types of text materials, and so forth; and unless all such variables are controlled, it is virtually impossible to attribute causality to one variable instead of another. What the Miami study allows us to conclude is that the students enrolled in the writing classes which used sentence-combining exercises outperformed students enrolled in a course which did not use those exercises. Whether the sentence-combining exercises did, in fact, increase performance is simply not known.

II. 4. *The University of Texas Study*

Although different in both scope and kind from the other three studies, the University of Texas study conducted by the present authors[20] complements certain aspects of the earlier three. Like all of the three previous studies, the Texas study attempted to measure improvement in the writing abilities of college freshmen across time. Like the other three studies, it examined the performances of students enrolled in a "traditional" freshman writing course. Like the San Diego study and the Northern Iowa study, it examined existing courses of study, rather than creating experimental ones. Like the Miami study, it compared the performance of students in a "traditional" course with that of students enrolled in a course predicated on sentence-expansion exercises.

The Texas study also differed in important ways from the other studies we have discussed. The Texas study, unlike the Miami study, did not hypothesize the greater efficacy of an "experimental" course over a "traditional" one. Neither course in the Texas study was considered experimental; both were courses which had been regularly taught for several years. Unlike the Miami study, however, the Texas study found significant improvement in the writing *and* reading skills of students enrolled in "traditional" freshman writing classes. Unlike the other studies, the Texas study examined changes in writing ability across two different types of writing, not just one.

But the most important difference is that the Texas study was based on a research design and analytic procedures that addressed the differences in instructional methods, curriculum, and instructional media in the courses compared. Our purpose in discussing the Texas study in some detail here is to illustrate the extreme difficulty in controlling major variables when two very different courses are compared.

II. 4. 1. Design and Results of the Texas Study

The Texas study compared the effectiveness of two options for the introductory freshman composition course, options which had been in place for several years. The two options for acquiring credit in the course differed with respect to instructional setting, method of instruction, instructional media, and curriculum. One option was taught in a conventional classroom while the second was taught in a laboratory. The first option relied on a combination of class discussions, some lectures, and individual student conferences, while the second relied almost exclusively on tutorials, with one teacher-tutor for every six students. The first option employed traditional, printed text materials, while the second used a combination of a programmed-learning text, a traditional text, and computer-assisted instruction.

The holistic option. Perhaps the most important differences between the two options lay in the instructional approaches to curriculum and in the theoretical assumptions which undergirded the two curricula. The first option employed what we call a *holistic* approach. It emphasized rhetorical and compositional principles in the context of whole pieces of discourse rather than in isolation. Based in part on the theoretical work of Kinneavy,[21] the option attended to the development of writing skills in the context of three purposes of written discourse—the expressive purpose, the persuasive purpose, and the referential purpose—as realized through Kinneavy's four modes of discourse—description, narration, classification, and evaluation.[22] The *holistic* approach was thus a top-down or whole-to-part approach to teaching composition. Students enrolled in the *holistic* option wrote the equivalent of six essays (500–650 words each), not counting the library paper, the journal, or two pretest and two posttest essays required by the evaluation design (see below). *The meristic option.* The second option employed what we call a *particle* or *meristic* approach. Rather than working from the whole discourse to the individual parts as in the *holistic* option, the *meristic* option approached the development of rhetorical and compositional skills in a deliberately synthetic way, working from individual discourse parts—in particular, sentences—to paragraphs and, finally, to multiple-paragraph essays. The rhetorical theory underlying this second option with its bottom-up approach was Christensen's generative rhetoric as adapted by Michael Grady[23] to the whole essay, and taught with further modifications through Wittig's *Steps to Structure*,[24] the major textbook in the course. The second option treated the sentence as the microcosm of the paragraph and the paragraph the microcosm of the essay. Accordingly, the assumption underlying this option was that skills developed in writing sentences could be synthesized into the larger, more complex skills required, first, in writing paragraphs and, second, in writing essays.[25] The students enrolled in the second option did not write nearly so many essays as did the students in the *holistic* option. In fact, they wrote only two besides the four essays collected as part of the evaluation. The students in the *meristic* option did, however, produce, through the large number of sentence and paragraph exercises, a number of words comparable to that produced by students in the *holistic* option.

If possible differences in student performance were to be explained, the curricular and instructional differences between the two options had to be accommodated in the research design. A design which factored out all of these differing components would have called for the examination of student performance in 42 different courses, only two of which would have been of primary interest. Instead, courses were constructed which would allow five principal comparisons across the two options.[26]

Five principal comparisons of the two options. The first principal comparison paired the two courses as they were normally taught, a comparison similar to the comparison used in the Miami study. The first principal comparison thus tested for *overall course effect.* The second principal comparison tested for the *effect of instructional approach* when the method of instruction was conventional class-room instruction for both options. In this comparison, both the *holistic* and the *meristic* options were taught in a conventional class-room setting. The *meristic* course examined in this comparison, un-like the course as it was normally taught, did not employ computer-assisted instruction. The third comparison tested for the *effect of the rhetoric text* on the *holistic* option with half the students receiv-ing rhetorical instruction through *The Writing Commitment* only and half receiving it through the course syllabus only. The fourth comparison tested for the *effect of instructional method*. Half the students received instruction via the *holistic* approach in a conven-tional classroom setting and half received it in a tutorial setting. The fifth principal comparison tested for the *effect of instructional ap-proach* when instructional method was always tutorial. The five principal comparisons are summarized in table 1.

Selection of students and teachers. Twenty beginning freshman composition classes (approximately 500 students) were selected for the evaluation study. The mean ECT scores for the students in these 20 classes did not differ significantly from the mean ECT scores for the students enrolled in the 160-plus classes of the same course of-fered that semester. Since we wanted to be able to draw conclusions that would apply to all classes and students in the first course in freshman writing, this test of comparability was mandatory. For each of the five principal comparisons four classes were used, two for each of the two sides of each comparison. By using two classes for either side of each comparison, we were able to ensure that no sub-group differed measurably from any other subgroup in the study. And when they were compared, the mean ECT score for any two-class subgroup used in the five principal comparisons did not differ significantly from the mean ECT score for all 20 sections in the study. Although the four classes for any given comparison were taught at about the same time during the day, time of day was not rigorously controlled across comparisons. For each principal comparison, two teachers were selected, with each teacher assigned one class on ei-ther side of the comparison. This procedure allowed us to control the teacher variable. By having the two teachers in each of the five principal comparisons teach one class on each side of the compari-son, we believed that if greater effectiveness were observed at the end of the term for one side of the comparison, that greater effec-

Table 1
Summary of the *Five Principal Comparisons* in the Texas Study

Compari-son No.	Section No.	Teacher No.	N of Students	Description	Tested Effect
1(a)	1	1	9	holistic/conventional	(Overall
	2	2	9	holistic/conventional	effect of
1(b)	3	1	9	meristic/lab-tutorial	course)
	4	2	9	meristic/lab-tutorial	
2(a)	5	3	9	holistic/conventional	(Effect of
	6	4	9	holistic/conventional	curriculum)
2(b)	7	3	9	meristic/conventional	
	8	4	9	meristic/conventional	
3(a)	9	5	9	holistic/conventional	(Effect of
	10	6	9	holistic/conventional	syllabus in
3(b)	11	5	9	holistic (syllabus)/ conventional	holistic curriculum)
	12	6	9	holistic (syllabus)/ conventional	
4(a)	13	7	9	holistic/conventional	(Effect of
	14	8	9	holistic/conventional	instructional
4(b)	15	7	9	holistic/tutorial	method)
	16	8	9	holistic/tutorial	
5(a)	17	9	9	holistic/tutorial	(Effect of
	18	10	9	holistic/tutorial	curriculum)
5(b)	19	9	9	meristic/tutorial	
	20	10	9	meristic/tutorial	

tiveness could not be attributed to teacher differences across the comparison.

Test procedures. The 500 students enrolled in the 20 classes were administered several measures pre and post to determine changes across the semester. During the first three or four class periods—depending on whether the class was taught on a Tuesday-Thursday or a Monday-Wednesday-Friday schedule—each student took the Miller-Daly Writing Apprehension Test (WAT),[27] the paragraph comprehension section of the *McGraw-Hill Reading Test*,[28] the *McGraw-Hill Writing Test*,[29] and two writing assignments—one on a topic which drew on personal experience and encouraged narrative and descriptive details and one on an argumentative topic. Two personal experience topics, the ones used in the Miami study, were used for the first of the two essays. One class on each side of each comparison wrote on one topic for the pretest while the other one on each side wrote on the other topic. For the posttest the topics were reversed. Two argumentative topics were used for the second essay, one on required literacy tests for high school seniors and one on required high school composition courses. For the pretest one class on each side of each principal comparison wrote on one argumentative topic and one on each side wrote on the other. For the posttest the topics were reversed.[30] Near the end of the term, students were given an opportunity to complete a course-instructor evaluation form widely used in composition classes at the University of Texas.

Analyses of data. From each of the 20 classes in the study, nine students who completed the course were randomly selected. The data collected from these 180 students were then submitted to detailed analyses. We analyzed each essay (720 in all) for length in words and for certain syntactic features. The four essays from each of the 180 students were coded to ensure student anonymity and to ensure that raters could not distinguish pretest essays from posttest essays. We then evaluated the essays holistically, with the 360 personal experience essays rated on one day and the 360 argumentative essays rated one week later. Each essay was given a score ranging from 1 to 4 by two raters. When the two scores differed by more than one point, the essay was submitted to a third reading to resolve the difference.[31]

Five derivative comparisons. In addition to the five principal comparisons, we created five derivative comparisons. These derivative comparisons drew on the data collected from the 20 classes used in the five principal comparisons. In these five derivative comparisons, controls over certain instructional variables were sacrificed in order to achieve larger "N's." The derivative comparisons were completed for the purpose of confirming the results of the five principal comparisons. The first derivative comparison pitted all *holistic* classes taught in a conventional classroom setting against all *meristic* classes taught in a conventional classroom setting. The second derivative comparison paired all *holistic* classes taught in a conventional classroom setting with all *meristic* classes taught tutorially. The third compared all classes taught in a conventional classroom setting with all classes taught tutorially. The fourth derivative comparison contrasted all *holistic* classes with all *meristic* classes. The fifth paired all *holistic* classes taught in a conventional classroom setting with all *holistic* classes taught tutorially. These five derivative comparisons are summarized in table 2.

The analyses of the data were performed in two stages: first, for the five principal and for the five derivative comparisons, and second, for all 180 students combined.

Principal and Derivative Comparisons. In spite of the carefully conceived research design, the principal and derivative comparisons in the Texas study yielded very few striking results. In Principal Comparison 1, which compared the two courses as they were normally taught, the analyses indicated that the holistic-conventional course produced greater gains in writing quality on the personal experience essays than did the meristic-laboratory-tutorial course. Although students on each side of each comparison improved in overall writing quality, this comparison was the only one that evidenced a difference owing to course effect. Significant improvement on both sides of each comparison made the courses in the remaining comparisons appear equally effective in promoting writing quality, regardless of type of writing. Principal Comparisons 1 and 2 indicated that the meristic curriculum produced longer argumentative essays, suggesting that the modified Christensen approach reflected in *Steps to Structure* helped developed invention skills. These essay length findings were confirmed by Derivative Comparisons 1 and 2. In addition, the fourth Derivative Comparison, which compared all holistic classes with all meristic classes, indicated significant gains for the meristic classes on the essay length of both the argumentative and the personal experience essays. The five principal and derivative comparisons also produced scattered syntactic differences that did not consistently favor either curriculum or any instructional method. No significant differences were observed for any of the standardized-test measures nor for the Writing Apprehension Test.[32]

Table 2

Summary of the *Five Derivative Comparisons* in the Texas Study

Compari- son No.	Section Nos.	N of Students	Description	Tested Effect
1(a)	1,2,5,6,9, 10,11,12, 13,14	90	holistic/conventional	(Effect of curriculum)
1(b)	8,9	18	meristic/conventional	
2(a)	1,2,5,6,9, 10,11,12, 13,14	90	holistic/conventional	(Overall course effect)
2(b)	3,4,19,20	36	meristic/tutorial	
3(a)	1,2,5,6,7, 8,9,10,11, 12,13,14	108	conventional	(Effect of instructional method)
3(b)	3,4,15,16, 17,18,19,20	72	tutorial	
4(a)	1,2,5,6,9, 10,11,12, 13,14,15, 16,17,18	126	holistic	(Effect of curriculum)
4(b)	3,4,7,8, 19,20	54	meristic	
5(a)	1,2,5,6,9, 10,11,12, 13,14	90	holistic/conventional	(Effect of instructional method)
5(b)	15,16,17,18	36	holistic/tutorial	

All students. Analyses of the pooled data for all 180 students showed a significant pretest-to-posttest change ($p < .037$) for only one syntactic variable, the percentage of words in final nonrestrictive modifiers in the argumentative essays. The length of the argumentative essays, a possible indication of greater invention skills, increased significantly ($p < .001$). Holistic scores for both the personal experience essays and the argumentative essays also increased significantly ($p < .001$) over the semester, thus suggesting that as a group the 180 students were actually writing better after one semester of instruction. As a group, the 180 students also significantly increased three of their four scores on the *McGraw-Hill Writing Test*: language mechanics ($p < .001$), sentence patterns ($p < .002$), and total score ($p < .001$). The gains on the reading comprehension part of the *McGraw-Hill Reading Test* were less dramatic but nonetheless significant ($p < .021$). The changes in reading comprehension scores were further explored by examining subsets of the data collected from the 20 classes. Using t-tests, we found that reading comprehension did not increase significantly for the *meristic*-conventional students ($N = 18$), the *meristic*-tutorial students ($N = 36$), the students ($N = 72$) enrolled in all classes taught tutorially, or the students enrolled in all the *meristic* classes ($N = 54$). However, significant changes were recorded by the students ($N = 90$) enrolled in all *holistic*-conventional classes ($p < .004$), the students ($N = 126$) enrolled in all *holistic* classes ($p < .017$), and for students ($N = 108$) enrolled in classes taught using conventional methods and in a conventional setting ($p < .019$). No significant changes were observed for scores on the Miller-Daly Writing Apprehension Test.

Additional analyses. In addition to looking at scores for essays and for multiple-choice tests of writing-related skills, we also examined student responses to an instructor-course evaluation instrument, interviews with some students, and the failure and attrition rates for the 20 classes.

The course-instructor evaluations were conducted using a 20-item instrument designed by a faculty-student committee at the University of Texas and administered through the Measurement and Evaluation Center. Although the results of this course-instructor evaluation are somewhat difficult to interpret for classes in which students saw several tutor-teachers during the semester, we could find no systematic differences in the evaluations of the various classes. One of the investigators also interviewed several of the students in the four classes used in Principal Comparison 1, which compared the two courses as they had been taught for several years. The only important difference between the two types of classes was heard in the comments the *meristic* students made about the problems they had adjusting to a course taught tutorially in a laboratory setting. Several of the *meristic* students interviewed indicated that they experienced considerable difficulty and frustration initially, but most remarked that after they had made the adjustment, they found the instructional method and setting to be a satisfactory alternative to regular class meetings and to group instruction by a single teacher.

Besides the course-teacher evaluations, we examined the failure and attrition rates of the 20 classes. We believed that the attrition rate would indicate whether the courses seemed to be meeting the needs and expectations of students enrolled in them. This examination proved to be very revealing. It showed that in classes taught in conventional classroom settings by teachers using conventional methods of instruction, the combined failure and attrition rate was under 10 percent or about two students for each of the 12 classes. The combined rate for failure and attrition jumped to about 25 percent for the eight classes taught tutorially. For the four *meristic*-tutorial classes, the combined rate was slightly over 34 percent. Since the rate for *meristic* classes taught in a conventional classroom setting with conventional methods of instruction was well under 10 percent, we inferred that the tutorial method was the cause of the higher attrition rate, not the *meristic* approach.

Text-internal measures and judgments of quality. In the five principal comparisons, we were concerned to discover, first, whether students' writing improved as a result of the writing instruction they received. Second, we were interested in determining whether certain text-internal changes might account for any increase in overall writing quality. We found no evidence that syntactic variables are predictors of the holistic scores of the 720 essays examined in the Texas study. In fact, in a series of multiple regression analyses, we found that in the personal experience essays, the best predictor of quality among the syntactic variables was the mean percentage of words in final nonrestrictive modifiers. And that variable predicted only 3.03 percent, leaving nearly 97 percent unexplained. On the argumentative essays, that variable predicted even less of the variance, 0.73 percent. And these were the best predictors among the syntactic variables we studied. Neither did essay length turn out to be a very good predictor, explaining only 4.94 percent of the variance in the holistic scores for the personal experience essays and only 6.52 percent in the scores for argumentative essays. Thus our cadre of text-internal measures of change or growth proved not to be terribly useful.

Writing apprehension. Using the data collected for the five principal comparisons, we also examined the relationship between writing apprehension and certain measures of writing ability and writing-related skills.[33] The results of these analyses suggest that writing apprehension is related to general verbal abilities and to writing performance. They also suggest that writing apprehension is linked to syntactic abilities. Our investigation showed that the low apprehensive students outperformed the high apprehensives on all essay measures at or beyond the .04-level of confidence, although the performative differences were less on the argumentative essays than on the essays based on personal experience. This latter finding suggested that perhaps the high apprehensive writers in the study performed better when the writing topic elicited a text not associated with the personal experience of the writer. Our analyses of the syntactic patterns of the high and low writing apprehensives in the study pointed to a tendency among high apprehensives to elaborate their statements less fully and to use the same syntactic constructions more frequently than low apprehensives. Low apprehensives were found to perform better on *The English Composition Test* (ECT) and on *The Test of Standard Written English* (TSWE), both measures which were administered to all students in the study before the beginning of the term.

The results of our analyses of the data collected for the evaluation suggested a number of conclusions. First, over the course of one semester, the 180 students as a group improved significantly on at least two types of writing. Second, as a group the students significantly improved their scores on two (not counting total scores on the *McGraw-Hill Writing Test*) objective measures of writing skills—language mechanics (grammar, punctuation, and spelling) and sentence patterns—and on one measure of reading ability—reading comprehension. Third, none of the classes affected either negatively or positively the amount of anxiety or apprehension the students experienced as writers. Fourth, even though Principal Comparison 1 suggests that students in *holistic* classes taught in a conventional setting wrote better personal experience essays at the end of the semester than their counterparts in the *meristic* course taught tutorially in a laboratory, none of the subsequent comparisons suggest that this difference can be attributable to either the greater efficacy of the *holistic* curriculum or the failure of the *meristic*. Subsequent comparisons—Principal Comparison 2, Principal Comparison 4, Principal Comparison 5, and the five derivative comparisons—

suggest that the difference may be attributed not to the curriculum but to the use of computer-assisted instruction. Fifth, since no definite causal relationship could be established between the holistic scores on either set of essays and the various syntactic indices or essay length, any changes along these dimensions, while often significant statistically, are probably meaningless. Sixth, the tutorial method of instruction appeared to be less effective in retaining students in freshman composition than did conventional methods. The tutorial method used in a laboratory setting was even less effective in this regard. Seventh, the use of computer assisted instruction appeared to affect adversely the performance of students enrolled in the *meristic*-laboratory/tutorial classes (Principal Comparison 1).

These seven conclusions allowed us to answer the two questions posed in most evaluations of writing courses and programs: Does the course or program seem to affect positively the development of writing abilities? and Is one approach to the teaching of composition more effective than another? The first question we should have to answer in the affirmative since the writing performances of all student groups examined appear to have improved significantly over the course of the semester and since the scores on most objective measures of writing-related skills also improved over the same time period. Because the students used in the study appeared not to differ from the freshman class at large and because there is no reason to believe that the teaching in the courses examined differed substantially in either quality or kind from teaching in other courses in the same program, our answer would extend beyond individual classes to the program itself. Our answer to the first questions, of course, entails some crucial assumptions about the validity of test instruments, both essay and objective.

Even allowing ourselves the luxury of the same assumptions, we can answer the second question only with less certainty. Both the *holistic* and the *meristic* approaches appear to enhance the writing abilities of their students, as judged by holistic evaluations of pretest and posttest essays on two very different writing assignments. The *holistic* approach appeared to do a slightly better job than the *meristic* in enhancing reading comprehension. Tutorial instruction, with which the *meristic* approach was associated in the program, appeared less effective than classroom instruction in retaining students.

II. 4. 2. Critique of the Texas Study

Although we believe the design of the Texas study to be superior to the other designs we have examined, the Texas study is not without flaw or limitation. One of the weaknesses lies with the size of the N's used in the principal comparisons. With an N of 18 on either side of each comparison, we can be confident that the significant effects observed are indeed significant; however, we have no assurance against Type 2 errors,[34] errors which occur when the size of the sample is too small to be certain that apparently nonsignificant differences are in fact nonsignificant. The problem of generalizing from the Texas study is compounded by the high attrition rate in the tutorial sections, particularly in those classes that taught the meristic curriculum. While the classes were judged equivalent at the beginning of the term, it is altogether possible that the weaker students and those students who would have negatively assessed tutorial instruction had dropped by the time of posttest. We see the loss of students over the course of a study as a major problem in a pretest-posttest design. For example, the Northern Iowa study finished with 12 percent of the students originally in the study.

A second weakness lies in the use of syntactic measures (e.g., mean clause length, mean t-unit length, mean percentage of t-units with final nonrestrictive modifiers, and mean percentage of words in final nonrestrictive modifiers). We analyzed these variables to provide definitive evidence on the relationship between syntactic maturity and writing quality among college writers. Because this relationship proved so slight, we were left with no measures to explain the variance in holistic scores. Another weakness was the use of a very general course-instructor evaluation instrument. The instrument used simply did not distinguish among teachers or classes in the study. Another weakness lies in the use of the *McGraw-Hill Writing Test*, a test selected because of its easy access but which is of questionable validity.[35] In addition, there are probably better instruments available for measuring reading comprehension than the *McGraw-Hill Reading Test*. Finally, we see as a weakness the amount of class time which was required to collect all the data mandated by the research design. At least some of that time might have been more profitably spent working with students on their writing.

Beyond the obvious limitations of such objective measures of "writing-related skills," other limitations of the Texas study are less obvious but more serious. From the start we attempted to overcome deficiencies we observed in previous evaluation studies (including our own). We attempted to examine a writing program from several perspectives, represented by the different measures employed. We did not, however, question certain fundamental assumptions about how to evaluate writing courses and programs. After two years of collecting and analyzing over 28,000 scores on various measures and categories, we discovered that we had found out little or nothing about what instructional practices or what composing practices brought about the higher holistic scores at the end. We began to question what we saw as the dominant model for evaluating writing courses and programs.

II. 5. *An Overview of the Dominant Quantitative Approach*

To the extent that the Northern Iowa study, the San Diego study, the Miami study, and the Texas study are representative (and we believe they are) of the designs and methods used in many evaluations of college writing programs, we can construct an evaluation model by focusing on the features common to all four studies. Most obviously, all four studies measured change across time and all involved comparisons. Indeed, it is impossible to envision an evaluation of any kind which does not involve explicit or implicit comparisons. In all four studies, comparisons were made across at least two groups of students, groups which apparently differed with respect to the way students were taught to write. The Northern Iowa study recognized two groups very broadly defined; the San Diego study posited four groups defined on the basis of large programmatic differences; the Miami study compared two groups within the same program; and the Texas study compared ten groups to one another. In all four studies, an evaluator's understanding of one group always depends on a concomitant understanding of the other group or groups examined.

A second shared denominator is that all four studies looked for changes in student performance across time, changes which tended to be attributed to the particular kind of writing instruction a given group had received. Changes in the performance of one group are interpreted in comparison with the performance changes in at least one other group.

These two common denominators point to a third feature which all four studies share. Evaluative judgments—whether of the effectiveness of different programs as in the San Diego study or of different courses within a program as in the Miami and Texas studies—of effectiveness are always relative judgments. That is to say, all four studies rendered judgments and drew conclusions which are at best valid for only the particular program. Thus for the Texas study, we can only claim that this or that group outperformed this or that group in the Texas study. We cannot conclude or claim that a given Texas group performed as well or better than, say, one of the groups in the Miami study. Similarly, while we may be able to assert on the basis of our evaluation of the Texas freshman program that the program is effective, we cannot claim that it is, for example, more or less effective than any or all of the four San Diego freshman "programs." In addition, since neither the San Diego, Miami, nor Texas study employed control groups which did not undergo writing instruction, none of these three studies can claim with certainty that the changes in student performance are solely attributable to this or that writing course.

In all four studies, judgments of the effectiveness of a given course in a writing program or the program itself are relative ones for still another reason. All four studies employed some form of holistic evaluation of pretest and posttest essays to determine the amount of change effected by a program. As we pointed out in our discussion of the San Diego study, holistic evaluations of essays are evaluations which are dependent on the total set of essays rated or scored at a particular time. Ignoring for the present the common set of essay topics used in both the Miami and the Texas studies, we can say that the writing topics differed across the four studies. In addition, there were probably some differences in student ability and in range of student ability across the four studies. Because research has shown that written products may differ according to purpose, mode, and topic[36] and that writers of differing abilities write differently, it is not possible to infer that a gain in holistic score of, say 0.60 in one study is comparable to a similar gain in another study, even when the scores are based on the same number of scoring categories.[37] Similar problems obtain when the same topics are used in different studies: even if populations are comparable to one another with respect to ability and ranges of ability, the scores are still dependent on the probably different criteria and processes by which raters arrived at their judgments. As Freedman's research shows, even slight variations in the ways holistic raters are trained can have significant effects on the ratings they give.[38]

Another feature common to all four of the studies we have reviewed is the reliance on products for evaluations of student performance (whether in the form of essays the students wrote or in the form of answers given to objective test questions) for judgments of program effectiveness. The dependency on products in the quantitative model involves a number of assumptions about writing instruction, about the development of writing ability, and about ways of measuring such development or ability. First, it assumes that the effects of writing instruction on students should be evident in the students' written products after only a very short time. Second, it assumes that controlled essays or objective tests are sensitive to whatever learning may have occurred because of the course. Third, such dependency assumes that the measures used are consonant with the goals of the course and program.

Each of these assumptions may in turn be challenged. It is possible to argue that even if the development of writing abilities is accelerated by means of instruction, growth along those dimensions which affect writing quality may occur so slowly as not to be meaningful after a relatively short time. Second, it could be argued that an instructional program in writing may affect the development of certain cognitive skills—such as the ability to classify—without having yet measurably or significantly affected the quality of students' written products. Third, it might be argued that an increase in the quality of written products may depend on the prior development of an understanding of rhetorical situations and the prior development of an awareness of and control over certain composing processes. A program may cause such understanding, awareness, and control without there being any immediate evidence in the student's written texts, especially those which are written under the contrived and artificial environment of a classroom or a testing center. Furthermore, composition instruction often increases the number of variables students must control as they make decisions during actual writing. A more highly developed awareness without a complementary development of control over composing processes may have an adverse affect on students' written products. The reliance on a model of evaluation which depends so heavily on the semester-end products may be a misplaced reliance.

Because of their disproportionate attention to semester-end products, pretest-posttest designs for writing program evaluation are inadequate for identifying and measuring changes in composing behaviors. They are also inadequate for evaluating what actually occurs in the classroom. In fact, many pretest-posttest studies do not consider this variable at all. In the two studies which attempted to assess teacher and course effectiveness—the San Diego and the Texas studies—the assessments were largely *post hoc* ones, dependent on students' recollections of things that had occurred several weeks or months earlier. None of the four studies made any attempt to observe or evaluate instruction systematically as it occurred, but all of the studies drew conclusions about the effectiveness of instruction. These conclusions amounted to inferences based largely on products collected at the end of the instructional period. For the same reasons that such products may not give a reliable or valid indication of growth in writing and writing-related skills, they may not have yielded valid or reliable bases for inferences about instruction.

Another characteristic of the quantitative model of writing program evaluation used to date is the assumption that the goals of the program are appropriate for the population served. In none of the four studies we reviewed were any rigorous attempts made to assess goals. Indeed, in none of the studies were specific goals even identified. The four studies simply assumed (1) that specific goals existed, (2) that they were appropriate for the student population served, (3) that these goals were being realized through the instructional methods employed, and (4) that they reflected adequately the larger contexts in which the programs and courses existed.

Furthermore, all four studies also ignored what might be called the logistical aspects of the programs and courses. None of the studies, for example, asked whether the structure of a program was a good one, whether it served adequately the needs of the students or the teachers. None of the studies tried to determine whether programmatic policies were being implemented in individual classrooms. None addressed the question of general teacher preparedness for teaching within a given program or whether the teachers adequately prepared for classes. None examined teacher-student ratios in an attempt to see whether the program or course was attempting too much or too little with the teaching resources available.

This overview of the four studies indicates the general nature of the quantitative model used in writing program evaluations to date. This model has at least the following characteristics: (1) it is oriented more toward products than it is toward processes, whether of composing or of instruction; (2) it usually attempts to measure changes in products over relatively short periods of time; (3) it provides for *post hoc* summative evaluations, evaluations which cannot change courses or programs while they are operating; (4) it produces findings which are for the most part local in their applicability; (5) it is predicated on several untested assumptions about the development and measurement of writing ability; (6) it does not examine the appropriateness of goals; and (7) it ignores program structure and administration.

Evaluation studies, including our own, which were based on the quantitative model have yielded few major insights concerning the teaching of writing or the operation of writing programs. Indeed, the findings of most evaluations of writing programs and courses hardly justify the massive efforts required to conduct the research. The implication for would-be evaluators of either writing programs or writing courses is clear enough: no matter how carefully conceived and constructed the design or how sophisticated the methods of analysis, evaluations must be based on more than pretest and posttest writing samples. Evaluations of writing programs and courses, if they are to result in valid and reliable judgments, must employ a variety of methods and procedures. Neither the expert-opinion approach to evaluation nor the pretest-posttest quantitative approach will alone suffice. Most importantly, evaluations of both writing programs and courses must proceed from a theoretical framework that can accommodate the complex workings of a writing program. In the following chapter, we outline such a framework.

3

A Framework for Evaluating College Writing Programs

AS THE FOUR STUDIES WE REVIEWED SUGGEST, THE COMPLEXITY of college writing programs has perhaps done more than anything to impede the development of adequate evaluation materials and procedures. If the quantitative model and the expert-opinion approach are inadequate, they are so, in part, because they fail to accommodate several important components of college writing programs and the complex relationships among these components. What is needed is a framework for evaluating college writing programs that can encompass their dynamic nature, a framework which will help overcome many of the weaknesses seen in the quantitative model of and the expert-opinion approach to writing program evaluation.

A framework which purports to address the evaluation of college writing programs must be able to do at least two things: it must specify the necessary components of writing program evaluation, and it must reflect the interactions among those components. These components and interactions determine the kinds of questions that evaluations can be designed to answer. In the present chapter, we identify and describe the major components of writing programs with which the evaluator must be concerned, as well as the interactions among them.

components + interactions

III. 1. *An Overview of Five Components of Writing Program Evaluation*

We contend that there are five general components of writing program evaluation. Within these five components are subsumed other components, several of which we discuss in the pages which follow. For the present, we will name and define briefly these five components. In subsequent sections of the present chapter we discuss the five components more fully.

1. *Cultural and social context.* Cultural and social context refers to the environment in which a writing program exists. It includes all influences from outside the institution which affect either the day-to-day operation of the program or the nature of the program. Cultural and social context might also be defined as that component of writing programs over which no one directly associated with the program has control.

2. *Institutional context.* This component refers to such matters as institutional policies and features which can affect different aspects of writing programs and the courses included in them.

3. *Program structure and administration.* This component refers to two important aspects of writing programs. First, it refers to the way writing courses are organized into a program. Second, it refers to all administrative aspects of the program not directly a part of an administrative structure beyond the writing program itself. Among the aspects of a writing program associated with administering that program are the following: teacher training and faculty development programs, common syllabi, provisions for and methods of evaluating faculty performance, and the logistics of delivering writing instruction and curriculum.

4. *Content* or *curriculum.* Content or curriculum is that which is taught in order for the program to accomplish its goals or objectives.

5. *Instruction.* This component refers to the methods or means used to teach the content or the curriculum of the program, in short, what teachers do to help students realize the goals of the program.

Each of these five components may interact with one or more of the other components. From the interactions among these five components, we can examine the *effects* of writing programs. Several points need to be made initially about effects. First, effects in writing programs may be either intended or unintended, but they always result from interactions among the five components. The intended effects of a writing program, like its curriculum, are likely to be reflected in the goals and objectives of the program. In contrast, unintended effects are never stated as goals or objectives. They are perhaps best described as unexpected or unanticipated, and they may be either positive or negative in nature. Unintended effects are more frequently identified by accident than by design. Second, whether intended or unintended, effects can also differ with respect to when they occur. Some important effects are observable only during the operation of the program; others may be "outcomes" evident only at the end of a term; still others may be long-range effects, such as subsequent academic, on-the-job, or social performance. This second point leads to a third: the effects of a writing program can be seen in its students, both during and after their formal instruction in writing; in its teachers; in its institutional context; and in its cultural and social context. Finally, effects can be seen in several kinds of data—among them written products, composing processes, and attitudes.

Each of the five components, together with a program's intended and unintended effects, generates questions which may be of interest to the evaluator of a college writing program. For example, the evaluator may need to determine whether the program is meeting the needs of the cultural and social context. The evaluator may also be called upon to determine whether any or all aspects of the program are, for example, compatible with the mission of the institution. Other evaluative questions might focus on the appropriateness of a program's curriculum or the instructional methods used to teach it. Answers to these questions—as we suggested in our review of the Northern Iowa, San Diego, Miami, and Texas studies—are most often discussed in terms of the effects of writing programs. By and large, the effects which evaluations of college writing programs have focused on are intended effects, usually measured through examinations of students' written products. Indeed, none of the four studies we reviewed provided for an evaluation of unintended effects.

The evaluator usually assumes that the first four components of writing program evaluation—*cultural and social context, institutional context, program structure and administration*, and *curriculum*—will remain relatively stable. Of course, the histories of many colleges and universities during the Viet Nam era illustrate how

contextual influences can change from day to day, as do school clos-
ings owing to natural gas shortages. In addition, unplanned changes
in program personnel, either administrative or instructional, may
result in administrative or curricular changes. *Instruction*, on the
other hand, is usually characterized by change since instruction is a
dynamic process. Teachers frequently change direction or tempo as
they adjust to the needs of particular students. Few teachers can
plan the instructional strategies of an entire term without having to
make adjustments before the end of the term. These changes contribute to the difficulty of assessing instruction, whether within individual courses or across courses within programs. Accordingly,
evaluators must be concerned with ways of describing and evaluating instruction as it occurs.

Insofar as a program seeks to alter the knowledge and performance
of its students, the program's *effects* may themselves be process-
oriented variables. Indeed, when later in this chapter we discuss
the *intended effects* of writing programs, we opt for the word *performance* instead of, say, the term *product* or the term *achievement*
to describe effects with reference to students in programs. Perhaps
from Tyler's early work on curriculum and evaluation,[1] the term
achievement has come to be associated in evaluation studies with a
model which is primarily concerned with static *products*.[2] It is this
"static products" or "outcomes" model which provides the underlying structure for the various National Assessments of Educational
Progress and for the competency testing movement.[3] The "static
products" model is also reflected in the quantitative method we
identified in our reviews in chapter 2 of the four evaluation studies.

But in a writing program, products are simply the results of performances or processes. In writing courses and programs, we believe as
much, if not more, attention ought to be paid to how products come
to be as to products themselves—that changes in processes of composing should be considered as legitimate an effect of writing programs as changes in the products of composing. It is not so much
that products are unimportant but that products in writing courses
are most meaningful when they are viewed as aspects of process-
oriented performances. The intended effects of a writing program
may also be reflected in the attitudes students hold—attitudes about
writing, about language in general, and about writing courses—as
well as in teachers' attitudes toward themselves and what they do.

To better understand how intended and unintended effects come about, we will take a closer look at the five major components of writing programs.

III. 1. 1. The Cultural and Social Context of Writing Programs

The *cultural and social context* is an extremely important component of writing programs, for it imposes certain restrictions or constraints on what the writing program can do. Cultural and social context affects the nature and the number of educational goals and objectives; it partly determines the curriculum taught; it influences how teachers teach and how effective they can be; and it contributes to student performance. The influence of the cultural and social context can be as substantial as dictating the specific goals of the program and as insubstantial as influencing the places where students can purchase text materials, as well the availability of those materials. The whole notion of a freshman composition program as a service to other academic departments derives in part from the influence of cultural and social context. In fact, a recent survey of writing program directors and teachers found that many of these academics thought society at large wanted them to serve society by producing students who could write "mechanically correct" prose upon graduation.[4] The "Back to Basics" movement probably was the direct result of the influence of social context on the teaching of writing in colleges and universities.

In the widest perspective, the context includes questions about the value and uses of literacy in a given society. Much recent work has examined these questions, for the most part looking at the effects of literacy in societies undergoing modernization.[5] But there has been relatively little work done on the functions of literacy in a modern, technological society or why college students should be taught composition skills.[6] In the first decades of the United States as a nation, writing was not so much essential to the working lives of Americans as it was to their social and political lives.[7] In contemporary American society, however, writing appears to be far more useful as a vocational skill than as a social skill, at least for college graduates.[8]

Other influences of the cultural and social context may be more subtle. In state institutions, for example, class size is often determined by the amount of money legislated for the operation of the institution. Another important aspect of context is the students attending an institution. Which students enroll in the courses in a writing program is often determined by policy- and decision-makers who are not themselves directly involved with the program itself. In state-supported institutions, legislators—sometimes in concert with administrative officials—determine which students and how many of them can be admitted to a particular college or university. The abilities of these students, as well as their own career goals, can influence the shape of a particular writing program. Postlethwaite cites evidence from the first National Assessment of Education Progress[9] of variations in the backgrounds of students which affect the ways students are able to learn, conditions which ultimately influence the way disciplines at the college level can be successfully taught.[10] A considerable body of research suggests that such contextual variables as students' academic fields can, independent of ability, affect the ways students approach tasks in other fields;[11] and Frederiksen's work on "task structure" indicates that strategies employed for different tasks may be determined both by the nature of the task and the students' ability,[12] which may differ according to educational or cultural background. In addition, Havighurst argues that the particular roles people play at different ages from preschool through retirement affect what they expect from education at different ages.[13] Anyone who has been privileged to teach older students with full-time jobs and families to support can appreciate the contextual influence which Havighurst identifies.

While it is not our purpose here to delineate the many ways[14] by which the larger cultural and social contexts of writing programs may influence the programs themselves, we do wish to illustrate the importance of these larger contexts. Perhaps the most obvious influence comes in the form of admissions policies. Virtually all educational institutions have altered their admissions policies within the last decade. The classic example of such policies—which, in turn, reflect cultural and societal values—directly influencing writing instruction is the case of the City University of New York. Once a university geared primarily to teaching students with above average academic preparation, CUNY, because of society-mandated changes in admissions policies, became responsible for teaching large numbers of underprepared students. When CUNY's admissions policy became one of open admissions, new ways of teaching students to write competently had to be developed. Out of this need to offer writing instruction to a substantially different student population came the now well-known work of Mina Shaughnessy[15] and a host of others.[16]

It seems to us that any comprehensive evaluation of a college writing program must explore the cultural and social contexts in which the program exists, for part of the effectiveness of a program is directly tied to the extent it is responsive to the cultural and social context. Only through the examination of larger contextual influences, which composition teachers and writing program directors often view as constraints, can one arrive at an adequate understanding of how and why the program operates as it does.

III. 1. 2. The Institutional Context of Writing Programs

The *institutional context* of a writing program may often be as difficult to pin down as its cultural and social context, because a writing program is itself a part of its institutional context, constantly shaping other features of the institution and constantly being shaped by those features.

Sometimes the institutional context can be seen as the constraints, both positive and negative, which are imposed upon the writing program by the institution in which it exists. Many of these "constraints" take the form of institutional policies; others are reflected in traditional practices, which may exist independently of any stated policies. As Rutman has argued, perhaps the best way for the evaluator to get a handle on the institutional context is to examine documents[17] which outline, among other things, the operating procedures of the institution. For instance, the evaluator may want to examine the institutional documents relating to the responsibility and authority of the writing program director to determine if the institution actually allows that administrator to direct the program he/she is responsible for.

In some cases, an examination of policy documents may lead to evaluative judgments directed at different aspects of the institutional context, judgments rendered in hopes of changing that context. One of the more common complaints offered by the writing program directors who responded to a recent national survey was that the attitude of tenured professors toward the teaching of writing fostered negative attitudes among junior colleagues and helped to keep the writing program at a second-class status within the department, usually an English department.[18] The second most commonly cited problem was the ineffectiveness of the administration of the writing program itself, an ineffectiveness caused, according to several directors, by the departmental limitations imposed on the positions they hold. Both of these problems suggest that whatever is wrong with the writing program itself can only be corrected by changing the basis on which faculty are rewarded and by changing the procedures under which writing program directors are forced to operate. In these two instances, an examination of the institutional documents—such as faculty promotion materials—may yield more than mere information that the evaluator could use as background for an evaluation of a writing program.

Institutional context can influence writing programs in more direct ways as well. The current interest in cross disciplinary writing courses also results, in part, from pressures brought to bear on composition programs from the outside, in this case academic departments that believe students may actually learn more about a subject by writing about it.[19]

Aspects of instruction are also subject to the influence of the institutional context. Although most of the research in this area has focused on instruction in elementary and secondary schools,[20] it is reasonable to assume that some of the same institutional influences affect teaching in postsecondary schools as well. Among these possible influences are the physical layout of the classroom, the attitudes within institutions toward the teaching of writing, the availability of duplication facilities and supplies, and the availability of facilities for conferences with students.

Adding to the complexity is the fact that a writing program can also shape the institutional context. For example, in many institutions all beginning freshmen are required to take writing courses. To the extent that these courses affect the way students perform in other courses, the writing program may be said to influence aspects of the institutional context beyond itself. Another potential source of influence is the size of most writing programs. In many institutions, the composition program offers more classes and uses more faculty than most major academic departments. Because of its size, the writing program may directly influence the way available resources are allocated within the college or university and may influence decisions and recommendations growing out of such groups as faculty councils and senates.

III. 1. 3. Program Structure and Administration

Program structure and administration is likely to present the evaluator with a number of difficulties. Most of these problems can be attributed to the fact that most college writing programs are in many respects unique, a point made repeatedly by directors who responded to a recent national survey.[21] Many of the directors surveyed believed that their particular programs were designed and are administered to accommodate the needs of particular kinds of students and particular kinds of faculty, thus making it difficult to discern important or substantive common denominators across different programs. Unlike writing program curricula, which often reflect differences in degree rather than kind across programs, program structure and administration can be unique to a particular institution. In some programs, for example, the writing program director may be responsible for creating and implementing programmatic policies; in other programs, the director may simply be charged with carrying out the policies handed down by, say, a department head or a curriculum committee. In some cases, writing program directors can determine which teachers will teach writing courses; in other programs, the director has no control over hiring practices at all. In some writing programs, teachers are allowed to teach whatever and however they wish; in other programs, teachers are required to follow a common syllabus which may dictate both curriculum and instruction. In some programs, directors are responsible for evaluating the faculty teaching in that program; in others, evaluation is conducted by administrators or faculty committees not associated with the program directly. In some cases, directors are very concerned about the relationships among courses within a program; in other cases, such relationships are not of great concern.

The point of all this is that *program structure and administration* are very difficult to describe with reference to other programs, primarily because this component of writing programs is most sensitive to the local circumstances. When generalizations across programs are either difficult or impossible, evaluation becomes even more difficult. Evaluators must not only spend considerable time describing this complex component, but they must then determine whether it is effective within the larger context.

III. 1. 4. Writing Curriculum: Focus on "What" and "How"

The *curriculum* of a given writing program may involve a number of curricular variables, primarily because writing itself is a complex activity demanding a larger number of goals and objectives. Because writing curricula are complex, Ryle's distinction between "learning that" and "learning how"[22] is extremely useful. Curricular variables may be classified either as *content* in the usual sense of a body of knowledge to be learned or as *content* in the sense of processes which can be applied or used to realize specific ends. In the courses which make up writing programs, curricular variables are frequently of both kinds.[23] Many writing courses have as one of their goals the teaching of different bodies of knowledge as well as teaching the act or process of writing. One body of knowledge consists of rules governing the use of punctuation marks, definitions of kinds and types of written discourse, lists of transition words, the concept of an essay or a paragraph. Other bodies of knowledge (e.g., literary genre, themes such as death and dying or humor) may provide the bases for *what* students can say analytically or interpretively about a written text. If a writing course curriculum requires students to analyze or interpret written texts, it delivers a *content* in the sense of *processes*, processes possibly quite different from those engaged during the act of writing. Such processes are, of course, themselves curricular variables. In conducting evaluations of writing courses or programs, it is always desirable and frequently necessary to recognize not only the curricular variables of the course or program but also the way or ways these variables interact with one another. For example, the students' knowledge of the history of the modern short story, their knowledge of the principles of literary analysis, and their knowledge of composing processes may interact in peculiar ways to produce better, or worse, freshman writers.

Elements of composition curricula have received much attention in the literature. Indeed, virtually everything ever said about *what* to teach in writing courses falls under the general rubric of *curriculum*. Subsumed under this general rubric is considerable diversity, much of which reflects a more-or-less traditional paradigm.[24] One useful way of understanding curricula is through the textbooks used, and perhaps followed, in the courses which make up the program. The importance of examining textbooks is suggested by our recent survey of writing program directors. In that survey we found great variation across types of institutions in the kinds of textbooks used in first- and second-semester freshman composition courses.[25]

William F. Woods, in a recent review article,[26] proposes a useful taxonomy for classifying college writing textbooks. Woods initially distinguishes between discipline- and student-centered texts, both of which make certain key assumptions about *what* is to be taught in the course. According to Woods, student-centered texts are generally expressionist in nature, stressing the natural development of the student's ability to express his/her thoughts and feelings in writing. According to Woods, "expressionist" texts regard all aspects of communication as extensions of the writer: language becomes the "'writer's voice,'" audience becomes the "'writer's inner ear,'" and logic becomes "'the writer's vision'" (p. 397). Discipline-centered texts, in contrast, are "interventionist"[27] in that they assume the individual needs to be shaped by cultural tradition. From this perspective, discipline-centered texts are either language-based (focusing on such matters as usage and style), rhetoric-based (focusing on traditional or modern concerns of rhetoric), or logic-based (focusing on the importance of clear thinking). Woods provides a number of subclasses under both language-based and rhetoric-based texts, but these subclasses need not concern us here; what is important is that while each type of text may have certain features in common with other types of texts, the differences among them may very well signal important differences in the curriculum of which they are a part. For example, if an "expressionist" text influences a writing curriculum, then one would expect students to do more writing from personal experience,[28] perhaps in the form of narrations, than they would if the controlling text were a discipline-centered text.

To distinguish among curricular elements on the basis of *what* and *how*, we may choose to view the components of a composition curriculum, as Frank J. D'Angelo does, in terms of an "underlying structure" for composition, a structure that "can be conceived of in terms of principles and forms."[29] D'Angelo argues that three sets of discourse principles and two sets of discourse forms provide this underlying structure. For D'Angelo three general categories of discourse principles—mechanical, linguistic, and rhetorical—underlie the teaching of composition. Each of these general categories itself contains several principles. Included under the rubric of "mechanical" principles are handwriting, capitalization, punctuation, and spelling. Within the class of linguistic principles, D'Angelo includes the principles of the word, sentence, paragraph, and essay; and three of the five classical divisions of rhetoric—invention, arrangement, and style—constitute D'Angelo's class of rhetorical principles. These three categories of discourse principles represent, according to D'Angelo, "the fundamental laws, rules, and conventions of discourse" and together determine "the intrinsic nature of discourse." In the hands of a writer addressing an audience for a purpose, these discourse principles combine to produce discourse forms and are themselves reflected in those forms. The forms of discourse can, according to D'Angelo, be either the traditional discourse modes—description, narration, exposition, and persuasion—derived from Alexander Bain [30] or the modern aims of discourse—expressive, persuasive, literary, and referential—as developed by Kinneavy.[31] D'Angelo's "underlying structure" of composition can serve evaluators as a very general guide for identifying certain of the curricular variables in a composition program, even though Bain's and Kinneavy's theories of "forms" are not as easily reconciled as D'Angelo suggests.

Other useful and important ways of viewing the forms of discourse composition curricula address appear in the work of Moffett,[32] the work of Britton and his colleagues at the University of London School of Education,[33] and the work being carried out under the auspices of the Council of Europe.[34] Moffett distinguishes between *kinds* and *orders* of discourse. These distinctions are based on the relationships among audience, writer, and subject. Moffett's orders are "interior monologue," "conversation," "correspondence," "public narrative," and "public generalization," a progression signaling increasingly greater distances between writer and audience. Moffett's kinds of nonfiction discourse are "drama," "narration," "exposition," and "argumentation," a progression which accommodates greater distances between writer and subject. Like Kinneavy's theory of aims and Moffett's theory of orders, Britton's theory of functions is predicated on changing distances, both physical and psychological, between writer and audience or among writer, subject, and audience. His progression of discourse functions may be represented as follows:

expressive discourse, poetic discourse, persuasive discourse, and informative discourse. Van Ek, working with the Council of Europe, specifies six general functions for users of the English language: "imparting and seeking factual information"; "expressing and finding out intellectual attitudes," "emotional attitudes," and "moral attitudes"; "getting things done (suasion)," and "socializing" (p. 25). It is important to note that these theories have several features in common with one another, features which suggest that the theorists are as much concerned with the act of discoursing as with discourse as a product.

Evaluating a writing program curriculum on the basis of discourse forms and principles may presuppose the prior knowledge of specific goals and objectives. If the specific goals and objectives of a course or program dictate that such principles and forms be taught either as content in the sense of *what* or as content in the sense of *how*, then curricular materials need to be examined carefully to determine how compatible they are with those goals and objectives.

III. 1. 5. Writing Instruction: Sequences, Methods, and Media

Instructional Sequences. Not only is it possible to examine and evaluate writing programs on the basis of the curricular components reflected in instructional materials, but it is also possible to do so on the basis of the way curricular components are sequenced for instructional purposes. Kinneavy[35] provides a useful system for examining composition instruction on the basis of the sequence of curricular elements. He offers a model of instruction that consists of eight components arranged around a circle representing instructional sequence. These components are "examples," "analysis," "principles," "environment and stimulus," "think," "write," "talk," and "rewrite." Not all of these components are, of course, present in every instructional situation. In what Kinneavy labels the "Traditional: Deductive Approach," which reflects the influence of classical rhetoric, especially Aristotle and Cicero,[36] the student begins by studying rhetorical principles, reads examples illustrating those principles, analyzes the examples, receives a writing stimulus, thinks, writes, perhaps talks about his/her writing, and perhaps rewrites. In the "Traditional: Inductive Approach," which echoes the practices of Isocrates, the curricular sequence is somewhat different: the student studies examples or models, analyzes the models, discovers their rhetorical principles, receives a writing stimulus, thinks about what he/she is to write, writes a piece, perhaps talks about the piece, and perhaps rewrites the piece.[37] Using these same eight components, Kinneavy outlines other approaches to teaching composition as well: "Example-Stimulus"[38] "Imitation,"[39] "Behavioral,"[40] and "Learn By Doing."[41] The point of all this is that instructional sequence can, and probably does, affect how students learn to write in a composition course. Organizational structures, such as those outlined by Kinneavy, reflect different assumptions about the way language skills are learned and should be taught.

Although other components may need to be added to Kinneavy's, we believe that different instructional organizations make different assumptions about the *content* or the *curriculum* of a writing course or program. A good illustration of this point is Christensen's "generative rhetoric,"[42] the instructional sequence for one of the courses examined in the Texas study. In generative rhetoric, one of the underlying assumptions is that sentences are structural microcosms of paragraphs and that paragraphs are structural microcosms of essays.[43] Because of its movement from parts of whole discourses (sentences) to larger units of discourse and, finally, to whole discourses, it is possible to describe the structure of a "generative rhetoric" course as *meristic*. Not all writing courses are, needless to say, so structured. In fact, Shuy has recently argued on theoretical and pragmatic grounds against what we have called the *meristic* approach.[44] Some writing courses are structured in just the opposite way, focusing first on the whole discourses to provide a textual context for exploring discourse particles. As in the Texas study, these courses might be termed *holistic* because of their whole-to-part orientation. Still other courses—probably most writing courses—fall somewhere in between the two extremes of meristic and holistic. The claim we wish to make is that the instructional organization of curricular components may affect the nature of the program itself and how well the students learn in a particular course within that program.

Identifying the usual patterns of instructional sequence is not difficult. The evaluator can usually identify sequence through such documents as program or course syllabi, instructional handouts, and assignment sheets. However, as far as we know, there are no altogether adequate methods for evaluating instructional sequence. One reason for the absence of adequate methods is the concomitant absence of research on instructional sequence in college-level writing courses. For example, we know of no convincing evidence that a *meristic* sequence is better than an *holistic* one, or vice versa. Although the Miami sentence-combining study and the North Dakota study of generative rhetoric *suggest* the greater efficacy of meristic sequences, the Texas study *suggests* that holistic and meristic sequences are equally effective for certain kinds of students.

We believe that the success of any instructional sequence may be directly contingent on the cognitive development of the students the sequence was implemented to serve. Some of the best research done on teaching writing to developmental students [45] has important implications for both writing curricula and the instructional sequencing of curricular elements in basic writing courses. We do not know, however, whether the same implications would hold for nondevelopmental students. The appropriateness of an instructional sequence must be determined, first, in relation to a writing curriculum, which begins in the elementary grades for individual students, and, ultimately, in relation to student performance. Instructional sequence is one area which could benefit enormously from a few carefully designed and controlled experimental studies.

Instructional Methods. If composition programs vary with respect to contexts, curriculum, and instructional sequence, they may vary even more so with respect to instructional methods. Indeed, Joyce and Weil have identified over 80 different models of teaching.[46] Some of these models are not, of course, ones which are widely used in composition teaching, but the point is that diversity in teaching practices can complicate writing program evaluation. This diversity can be attributed, in part, to personality differences among teachers.[47] In the teaching of composition, one of the most commonly used methods of instruction is that which might be labeled as "traditional classroom discussion"; but even within that general method can be found considerable variety. For example, the discussion method is frequently supplemented by student conferences or writers' workshops. And within the area of discussion, methods may vary considerably. Recently, one of the present authors visited two writing classes, each taught by a different graduate student enrolled in a practicum on teaching freshman composition. In both classes, discussion centered on assigned readings illustrating the principles of classification. In one class, the teacher led the discussion from a set of questions she had prepared over the readings, questions focusing on classification systems and membership in classes illustrated in the readings. Students responded by attempting to answer the questions directly, and discussion ensued only when a particular response to a question was deemed unsatisfactory. In the other class, the general instructional method was also discussion, but the form of the discussion was more obviously inductive, with the teacher deriving each subsequent question from student responses to previous questions. While both classes may be labeled as discussion classes, the actual discussion practices and procedures differed substantially. The problem that writing program evaluators have to face is that if the two classes are compared on the assumption that both employed like instructional methods and one course proved more effective in teaching the principles of classification, that difference in effectiveness could be attributed to the two different methods of conducting class discussions. The evaluator must, therefore, be sensitive to what may seem to be subtle differences in instructional methods.

In the teaching of composition, a large number of nontraditional methods are also frequently used, many of which have received documentation in the literature. Reflecting both curricular and instructional concerns, one useful recent summary of classroom practices in the teaching of writing suggests that modern composition classroom practices put greater emphasis on "cooperating in the process of writing rather than on criticizing the products of composing"[48] than did the practices of earlier years. This shift in emphasis in classroom practices—which also reflects corresponding shifts in *curricula* and *contexts* and makes different demands on program *administration*—may be attributable, in part, to the influence of the Dartmouth Conference with its concern for classroom interaction and activities of learning.[49] At any rate, the result of this shift in emphasis has been the development of new instructional methods. Of these new methods—most of which focus on writing processes— two will serve to suggest some of the problems such methods pose for the evaluator of writing courses.

One widely publicized method is the one advocated by Murray.[50] This method, as described by Murray and Carnicelli, involves conferencing with individual students about their writing as it is being written. The conferences are presumably conducted so that the focus of attention is always on the students' writing, with the teacher serving as a guide to help students through the writing process.[51]

A second relatively new instructional method falls under the general rubric of collaborative learning, which includes the notion of peer tutoring as outlined by Garrison[52] and as popularized by, for example, Bruffee.[53] Like the conferencing approach to writing instruction, collaborative learning places a greater emphasis on the processes involved in composing. When the collaborative model is used, students presumably have ready access to peers for responses to their written products and for consultation as drafts are being written. Both the conferencing approach and the collaborative approach would seem, by their very nature, to encourage student writers to develop a sense of the audience that will be reading and responding to the texts they produce.

While these two approaches, two instructional methods, to teaching writing are widely known and often used in college writing courses,[54] considerable variety is possible within both. For people interested in writing program evaluation, these variations within general classes of instructional methods are perhaps no less important than differences between the classes themselves. We have seen peer tutoring, for example, used in a number of different ways—as a part of a writing course primarily dependent on more traditional instructional methods, as a part of a laboratory course in which peer tutoring supplements the instruction offered by the teacher of record, and as the only means of providing students with evaluations of the written texts they produce. So too with conferencing. Our concern here is, of course, the concern of the evaluator for describing accurately instructional methods used in writing courses. Rarely, in evaluating instruction in any discipline is it sufficient to say that a course was taught according to this or that general model of instruction. Accurate descriptions of instructional methods used in college writing courses and programs must precede evaluations of them.[55]

Instructional Media. The components of writing curricula and the instructional methods used to teach writing curricula must not only be kept separate from one another in the evaluation of a writing program, but they must also be distinguished from instructional media. Instructional media may be thought of as delivery systems, and they interact in the classroom with both curricular components and instructional methods. Until recently, composition specialists needed to be concerned primarily with but two instructional media, the printed word and the spoken word. Now, composition specialists have to be concerned with other media as well. It is becoming increasingly common in composition courses, for example, to use television shows and motion pictures to provide the content for student writing or to illustrate various principles of communication.[56] It is also becoming more common in some quarters to use computers both to teach students conventional usage and to assist them in the actual writing of essays by providing for interactive use programs in invention or essay structure and development.[57] As in the use of instructional methods, considerable variety exists in the use of instructional media, even in the ways a particular medium is used. Again, it is not sufficient in writing program evaluation simply to identify courses which use computers, because what is important is the precise way computers fit into the course itself and the purposes for which they are used.

III. 2. *The Effects of Writing Programs*

Virtually all evaluations—whether of writing programs or of anything else—have to be concerned with effects. In evaluating writing programs, we must be concerned with the many ways those programs affect people—the students, the faculty, and even the society at large. In the four evaluation studies reviewed in chapter 2, the effects of writing programs were evaluated almost exclusively in terms of students' written products. As we pointed out, however, preoccupation with written products in writing program evaluation has resulted in a narrow definition of student performance—one at odds with much of the current research on composing.[58] In addition to looking for programmatic effects within student products, evaluators must also examine changes in the attitudes of both students and teachers brought about by the day-do-day operation of the program. The preoccupation with student products has diverted attention from not only the intended effects of a writing program as expressed through statements of goals and objectives, but has also obscured the unintended effects of writing programs. It is important for evaluators to realize that whether the source of data is products, processes, or attitudes, the effects they measure may be either intended or unintended.

The *intended effects* of a college writing program are typically either expressed or implied in statements of *goals*. Ideally, these statements serve as links between *contexts* on the one hand and *curriculum* and *instruction* on the other. One of the tasks of the evaluator of any program—whether a writing program or a football program or a program for aid to dependent children—is to determine what the program is supposed to achieve, its *raison d'être*. Unless the intended effects of the program are known, it is impossible to determine whether they have been realized. A second evaluative task, then, is to determine whether the effects intended were actually produced. Since some effects may be unintended, a third evaluative task is to identify those which occurred.

Intended Effects. The literature on evaluation suggests two approaches to identifying the objectives of a program. The least used is the goal-free model of evaluation proposed by Scriven.[59] As House points out, Scriven's concern with goal-free evaluation is a concern for the reduction of bias.[60] Scriven has argued that if informed of the goals of a program in advance of the evaluation of it, the evaluator will likely overlook important "side effects," what we have labeled unintended effects. As Scriven puts the matter, "it's risky to hear even general descriptions of the intentions [i.e., the goals or objectives] because it [sic] focuses your attention away from the 'side effects' and tends to make you overlook or down-weight them."[61] Employing Scriven's goal-free approach, an evaluator would discover the goals, both the stated and the unstated, during the course of the evaluation itself.

Scriven's arguments in favor of goal-free evaluations notwithstanding, most evaluators try to identify the goals and objectives of the program during the beginning stages of the evaluation. Although most writing programs appear to operate on the basis of goals and objectives, statements of them are typically very broad and very general and, therefore, of limited value in determining the exact nature of the program or the courses within a program. Broad, general statements of goals have much more in common with statements of good intentions than they do with specific, observable aspects of writing programs. Most writing program directors and most teachers of writing, for example, see the major goal of freshman writing programs and courses as the improvement of student writing.[63] However important such statements may seem, they provide the evaluator with very little information useful in conducting an evaluation.

What the evaluator needs are statements of specific goals and objectives. It is usually over the specific goals and objectives of a course or program that teachers and writing program directors disagree, even though they may agree on the general goals and objectives.

For an evaluation to be useful, it seems to us that teachers and writing program directors must agree in advance of the actual evaluation on the specific goals or objectives of the writing program and of the courses included in that program, especially as those goals and objectives immediately affect students enrolled in the program. Getting agreement is, however, frequently difficult. Indeed, a recent national survey of teachers' and directors' perceptions of the goals of freshman writing programs indicates considerable disagreement between the two groups on the matter of goals;[64] and that survey combined with a survey of the writing college graduates[65] indicates that neither writing program directors nor teachers may perceive the same goals for college writing programs as people who have graduated from college. While meetings with the teachers and the writing program director may help the evaluator identify some of the specific goals and objectives, it is unlikely the group will arrive at consensus, except through the influence of dominant and dominating personalities. Weinberg explains the problem and recommends a solution:

> Now committees in my view can no more produce wisdom than they can design a camel. The atmosphere of a committee is too competitive, too verbal. Wisdom is a very personal kind of thing: it flourishes best when a single mind thinks quietly and consistently—more quietly and consistently than is possible when one is engaged in the rough-and-tumble of committeeship with its often tendentious and personal exchanges. Thus, I have felt that some of the most troublesome questions ought to be thought through by individuals who would then set thoughts down in essays. Out of many such essays, written by different people, could come, if not clarity and guidance, at least a common language in which to conduct the discourse.[66]

Such written responses could be analyzed for content,[67] for different statements of specific goals and objectives. These statements could then be used in connection with the Delphi technique.[68] The Delphi technique involves collecting statements, such as those suggested by Weinberg, summarizing them, and then circulating the summary. The group, in this case the teachers and the writing program director, is then asked to re-evaluate their positions on goals and objectives in light of the summary document and then to submit another statement. These new statements are again summarized, the summary circulated, and revised statements again collected. The process continues until consensus is reached.

The goals and objectives for student performance, of course, can be of many kinds. And whether the Delphi technique or some other method is used to identify them, the evaluator—as well as the teachers and the writing program director—must be able to group or classify those goals and objectives. One classification system that frequently appears in the literature on educational goals and objectives identifies cognitive,[69] affective,[70] and psychomotor[71] goals and objectives. The usefulness of these three divisions may be that they allow goals and objectives to be classified according to a consistent framework which uses a vocabulary most teachers and writing program administrators are already familiar with. In addition, it allows an evaluator, or a group of persons associated with an evaluation, to determine what might be called the "balance" among the different types of goals and objectives. Although there are inherent weaknesses in any taxonomy, composition programs and courses probably have goals which address the cognitive and affective domains of the learner. And the more general of these goals are often stated in one form or another—in college catalogues, in writing program policy statements, and in course syllabi. Less obvious, and less prevalent, are psychomotor goals, for most college programs simply assume that students have command of the psychomotor skills necessary for them to perform adequately.[72]

Other taxonomies can also be used to classify the goals and objectives of college writing courses and programs that bear on student performance. As Yow points out,[73] Gagne's categories of learning—chaining (i.e., stimulus-response), verbal association, multiple discrimination, concept learning, principle learning, and problem solving—can be used to classify the goals and objectives of an educational program.[74] The three higher level categories—concept learning, principle learning, and problem solving—seem particularly relevant to many of the goals and objectives of writing programs and courses. These same goals and objectives might also be classified according to Vygotsky's stages of concept formation.[75] Vygotsky distinguishes among three such stages: (1) the putting "together a number of objects in an *unorganized congeries*, or 'heap,' in order to solve a problem that we adults would normally solve by forming a new concept" (p. 59); (2) "*thinking in complexes*" during which "individual objects are united . . . not only by . . . subjective impressions but also by *bonds actually existing between these objects*" (p. 61); and (3) using true concepts (pp. 61–118). It seems to us that many instructional activities—such as the different kinds of sentence combining exercises—might be placed at the different "cognitive" levels suggested by Vygotsky's stages of concept formation. Piaget's stages of mental development might also be used as the basis of a taxonomy of goals and objectives for writing programs and courses. Piaget distinguishes among four such stages—the sensori-motor, the pre-operational, the concrete operational, and the formal-operations stage.[76] Also potentially useful is the well-known distinction Chomsky makes between competence and performance.[77] This distinction is, in fact, applied in a modified form to performative goals and objectives by the contributors to *The Nature and Measurement of Competency in English.*

We have argued above that evaluation studies typically take the written texts of students as the primary evidence of the effects of writing programs. The assumptions underlying this practice are three: (1) that students' written texts collected under testing conditions are adequate reflections of writing competency, (2) that legitimate inferences about writing course and program effectiveness can be made on the basis of student texts, and (3) that writing programs only affect student products. Evaluators have come by this practice quite naturally: the country's writing assessment experts—the National Assessment of Educational Progress and the Educational Testing Service—use the written texts of students to make inferences about writing competency and program effectiveness.[78] In addition, it is a practice used by most classroom teachers of writing to judge both the competence of student writers and to gauge the effectiveness of writing instruction. Most evaluation studies—including the four evaluation studies we reviewed in the previous chapter—base most of their conclusions on students' written products. Implicit in all of these evaluations—from individual classrooms to national attempts at writing evaluation—is the assumption that written products represent the "bottom line" in assessing student performance and writing course effectiveness.

In large-scale evaluations, two kinds of student products have been assessed: student responses on standardized tests of writing-related skills and actual writing samples. Standardized tests are used in indirect assessments of writing, and writing samples are the basis of direct assessments. There are strengths and weaknesses in both forms of assessment. Proponents of indirect assessments argue that standardized instruments are more reliable than direct assessments and less expensive to administer. Critics of indirect assessments, on the other hand, question the validity of such instruments as measures of writing ability since examinees usually write no more than their names. Proponents of direct assessments argue that the only valid measure of writing competency is a writing sample, in spite of the fact that they are relatively expensive and difficult to score and that they predict success in writing courses no better than indirect assessments.[79]

But validity can be questioned in direct assessment as well as indirect assessment. In recent times the issues of validity in direct assessment has usually been raised with respect to the number and kinds of writing samples required to assess competency.[80] Further questions can be raised about the kinds of cognitive abilities direct assessments measure and the writing tasks themselves. The NAEP, for example, once asked students to write in response to the following questions: "What would it be like to be a goldfish? Or an airplane? Or a horse? Or a tree? Or any other thing?"[81] What is being measured with this assignment? The students' ability to use their imaginations? To communicate with a "real" audience? To show their knowledge of goldfish, horses, or whatever?

Perhaps a more critical question bearing on the validity of direct assessments is their inability to assess writing processes adequately. Indeed, most direct assessments require that students write in very limited time span on an impromptu topic, a topic about which some of the examinees may have a great deal of knowledge and others may not. This procedure runs directly counter to what we know about how experienced writers compose.[82] If writers do not have command of the requisite prior knowledge to write about a subject, then they must have the time to generate ideas on that topic. In any case, most direct assessments do not provide adequate indications of skills in invention. Furthermore, direct assessment does not allow for substantial revision, for adjusting a text to the needs of a "real" audience if one were provided.

Following the lead of numerous researchers who have studied composing processes, many writing teachers now believe they follow a process-oriented curriculum.[83] Both indirect and direct assessments of writing tell us very little about how students' composing processes might change as the result of instruction, about whether a student who habitually stops thinking about a paper at the end of a single draft might be willing to take a paper through multiple drafts.

Thus products alone may not give an adequate picture of writing competency. Nor can products alone give adequate information about the effects of writing programs. While writing programs have traditionally sought to improve the quality of written products, programs produce other important effects as well. For example, some writing programs and many writing teachers have as a goal the development of cognitive abilities that allow students to perform better in courses in other disciplines. Indeed, many writing programs claim to teach intellectual processes—such as induction, deduction, and classification—which are fundamental to all academic disciplines and are believed to affect the performances of people after college. Some students, both during and after writing instruction, may be able to use skills in reading and thinking without employing them in writing, thus making direct assessments of writing perhaps inappropriate indicators of certain intended effects of a writing program. In addition to developing control over composing and other cognitive processes, composition programs also sometimes aim to produce changes in attitudes which are not reflected in written products during the term of the course. For at least some students, a change in attitude toward writing may be just as important as improvement in written products. Students who fear writing have been shown to avoid courses and jobs that require writing.[84] Moreover, writing programs often seek to increase students' appreciation of written language as a medium of communication and means for self-expression. These effects may not only be inaccessible through assessments of written products but may not even occur until sometime after students have completed their formal courses in writing.

Unintended Effects. Not only must program evaluators be concerned with identifying the intended effects of writing programs and courses, but they must also take into account the unintended effects. One of the best examples of unintended effects is the negative attitude toward writing that many students bring to the writing classroom. Many college teachers attribute these attitudes to error-oriented instruction in previous courses dealing with writing regardless of discipline. Other unintended effects may be the development of misconceptions about writing, both as product and as process. Some of these misconceptions center on writing processes —such as writing is easy for good writers or that good writers get it right the first time. Others center on products—such as every paragraph should start with a topic sentence or that good writing always reads like an essay by George Orwell or E. B. White. Not all unintended effects concern students. For example, the required use of a common syllabus in a particular writing course may cause teachers to alter their teaching practices to such an extent that they feel they lose their effectiveness. The number of papers that teachers are required to grade according to program policy during a term may adversely affect morale in a department. Writing programs have other unintended effects beyond their immediate confines. Because English departments have traditionally taught most writing courses, responsibility for teaching writing has been shunned in other departments, a situation which is changing in many institutions. Finally, writing programs—for good or bad—have had some responsibility in shaping attitudes toward language and writing held by the public at large.

III. 3. *Interactions Among the Five Components*

As we intimated in previous sections, writing program evaluation must necessarily be concerned with the effects of writing programs. Which effects are important depends on the way the evaluator chooses to view the writing program and what questions need to be answered. As we have seen, writing program evaluators can choose, for example, to limit the scope of an evaluation to an examination of the effects of a particular instructional method on students' written products. Such an evaluation entails a monistic view of writing programs, with respect both to effects and to possible causes. That is to say, such an evaluation is unidimensional in nature, while the writing program being evaluated is multidimensional, consisting at least of a cultural context, an institution context, program structure and administration, a curriculum, as well as a pedagogy.

To evaluate a writing program unidimensionally is to engage in an activity similar to the examination of the elephant by the six blind men. If the evaluator examines only the "trunk" of a writing program, the interdependence of all the parts will be missed. Whatever the elephant does, it does because its several parts work in concert with one another in a particular environment. So too with writing programs: no single component can be singled out for examination if the evaluation truly seeks to understand the cause or causes of this or that effect. Evaluators must be aware of the ways the five components can combine, or interact, to cause certain effects.

If we consider all the possible combinations of the five components, there result 26 possible sets of interactions which deserve the evaluator's attention. In the most comprehensive evaluation, the evaluator would look for the causes of particular effects in the complex interactions among the cultural context, the institutional context program structure and administration, the curriculum, and instructional methods. In less comprehensive evaluations, one or more of the 25 lesser interactions would be of importance:

1. cultural and social context with institutional context,

2. cultural and social context with program structure and administration,

3. cultural and social context with curriculum,

4. cultural and social context with instruction,

5. institutional context with program structure and administration,

6. institutional context with curriculum,

7. institutional context with instruction,

8. program structure and administration with curriculum,

9. program structure and administration with instruction,

10. curriculum with instruction,

11. cultural and social context with institutional context with program structure and administration,

12. cultural and social context with institutional context with curriculum,

13. cultural and social context with institutional context with instruction,

14. cultural and social context with program structure and administration with curriculum,

15. cultural and social context with program structure and administration with instruction,

16. cultural and social context with curriculum with instruction,

17. institutional context with program structure and administration with curriculum,

18. institutional context with program structure and administration with instruction,

19. institutional context with curriculum with instruction,

20. program structure and administration with curriculum with instruction,

21. cultural and social context with institutional context with program structure and administration with curriculum,

22. cultural and social context with institutional context with program structure and administration with instruction,

23. cultural and social context with institutional context with curriculum with instruction,

24. cultural and social context with program structure and administration with curriculum with instruction,

25. and institutional context with program structure and administration with curriculum with instruction.

These interactions are vital to understanding the effects of a particular program. In any given interaction, the evaluator can look for the effects of one component on another or of two, three, or four components on another component. In the next chapter, we will discuss how these components and the interactions among them lead to evaluation questions which require the use of multiple methodologies.

4

Accommodating Context and Change in Writing Program Evaluation

THROUGHOUT THE PREVIOUS THREE CHAPTERS, WE HAVE SUG-gested that the complexity of writing programs has done much to limit the development of adequate evaluative procedures and methods. Yet the sheer complexity of the thing evaluated is not the only reason the art of writing program evaluation remains in its infancy. The nature of evaluation itself raises many questions and issues that should be reexamined in every significant evaluation. We have in mind those evaluations which have the potential to affect the lives of others, the kinds of serious evaluations in which evaluation itself is often an issue. Usually these questions focus on the validity of the evaluation. Such questions certainly arise when evaluation is misused covertly in the ways outlined by Suchman—as a way to "eyewash" in order to call attention to only the good aspects of an otherwise poor program; as a way to "whitewash" in order to hide a program's failure; as a way to "submarine" a program regardless of its worth; as a way to create the appearance or "posture" of objectivity; and as a way of postponing administrative action under the pretence of insufficient facts.[1] Yet questions of validity have been raised about even the most conscientiously conducted evaluations, whether of writing programs[2] or of social and educational programs generally.[3]

As we indicated in chapter 1, our central concern in the present monograph is with validity in writing program evaluation. Our discussion in chapter 2 of the Northern Iowa, San Diego, Miami, and Texas studies focused on matters which bear on the validity of those evaluations. And in our discussion of the quantitative model of writing program evaluation, we tried to point out the inherent weaknesses and limitations that reduce the validity of results generated. In the third chapter, we presented the major components of a theoretical framework for conducting valid evaluations. We argued that this framework accommodates or accounts for the five necessary components of college writing program evaluation: the cultural and social context of the program, its institutional context, its structure and administration, its curriculum, and its pedagogy. At the end of chapter 3, we suggested that writing program evaluators must look to complex sets of interactions among those five components in order to develop a comprehensive view of a program and its effects, both intended and unintended. The first three chapters of the present monograph thus define the "territory" affecting validity in writing program evaluations.

Validity is the central issue addressed in the present chapter as well. Validity depends on the appropriateness of the evaluation to the nature of the thing evaluated. In the following section we address briefly the development of and the need for two distinctive approaches to evaluation. In the second section, we point out how changes in writing programs and in conceptions of writing require new evaluation procedures and materials. In the third section, we suggest directions which research must take in order to develop valid procedures and materials for evaluating writing programs.

IV. 1. *Quantitative and Qualitative Methods in Evaluation Research*

Whatever virtues or vices may be discussed with respect to evaluation, the issue of validity is always present. Questions about the validity of a writing program evaluation are often raised because the data examined and the analytic methods and paradigms employed are often distrusted by persons who have a professional interest in the teaching of college writing. Part of this distrust stems, of course, from the backgrounds of college faculty who are charged with the teaching of writing. Such persons often have strong literature backgrounds[4] which better prepare them to analyze single written texts than to analyze enormous amounts of data collected under more or less controlled conditions. The research method familiar to most teachers of writing is the method of the literary scholar who confronts a text one-on-one, and from such a one-on-one meeting discovers certain truths about life, the human condition, and art. As Eisner has recently argued, there is much to be said for "artistic approaches to research," approaches which try, as literary scholars must do, "to locate the general in the particular." Eisner continues: "[such approaches] attempt to shed light on what is unique in time and space while at the same time conveying insights that exceed the limits of the situation in which they emerge. This is precisely what Aristotle meant when he said that 'Poetry' was truer than history."[5] Yet while there is much value in employing evaluation methods comparable to those of the literary scholar, it is often impossible to conduct a comprehensive evaluation of a large program or even a single course using exclusively those methods. Evaluations of writing programs cannot concern themselves with individual performances only, performances which may or may not be generalizable; they must be concerned with the performances of large groups of students and often with large groups of teachers, a circumstance which may demand a combination of several methodologies.

There are good reasons, however, for distrusting the quantitative aspects of evaluation, for as we pointed out in our review of the four studies, quantitative methods do not necessarily produce useful or valid results or even reliable results. Thus, a central issue is the extent to which evaluation should be regarded as a science. Some researchers, for example, have maintained that qualitative methods and models are highly questionable, as have Campbell and Stanley in their classic work on research design. Addressing one particular qualitative method, Campbell and Stanley write that the case study approach typifies "the error of misplaced precision" and that "It seems well-nigh unethical at present to allow, as theses or dissertations in education, case studies."[6] Very recently, the quantitative bias of Campbell and Stanley has been reiterated by Rossi and Wright: "There is almost universal agreement among evaluation researchers that the randomized controlled experiment is the ideal model for evaluating the effectiveness of public policy. If there is a Bible for evaluation, the Scriptures have been written by Campbell and Stanley."[7] Yet even Campbell,[8] as well as other such noted quantitative researchers as Cronbach,[9] now apparently finds qualitative methods more acceptable. Speaking directly to the concerns of the evaluator, Kemmis addresses the quantitative/qualitative distinction in the following way:

> Too often evaluators assume that their clients want them to collect a body of "objective" test data so that the clients can make decisions about educational programs; it is assumed that these decisions follow by implication from the evaluation data. In their sophistication, the evaluators may forget that the data they give to their clients create only a bare skeleton of the many-sided reality of the program. It is cold and unyielding to the technically inexpert eye; it does not adequately render the living reality of people, events, and issues in day-to-day program operation. Furthermore, the reality it does create, that of outcomes achieved and not achieved, presented in scores, tables, and graphs, may actually *mislead* program personnel insofar as it leads them to value those things that the evaluator *can* measure at the expense of those aspects of the situation too elusive to be captured by his measurements.[10]

One of the fundamental differences between quantitative and qualitative methods is the role of the researcher: in a quantitative study, the researcher stands apart from the object of study, but in a qualitative study, the researcher becomes something of a participant, intent on being able to represent the complexity of the activities under study.

But this difference between the roles evaluators play in quantitative and qualitative approaches to evaluation is not to be taken lightly as a simple difference in procedure. Quantitative and qualitative methods embody fundamentally different theories about both the nature of reality and about the nature of knowledge and knowledge acquisitions. Patton, one of the better known authorities on evaluation, contrasts the two methods and indicates the historical evolution of the two often competing paradigms:

> Evaluation research is dominated by the largely unquestioned, natural science paradigm of hypothetico-deductive methodology. This dominant paradigm assumes quantitative measurement, experimental design, and multivariate, parametric statistical analysis to be the epitome of "good" science. This basic model for conducting evaluation research comes from the tradition of experimentation in agriculture, which gave us many of

the basic statistical and experimental techniques most widely used in evaluation research. . . .

By way of contrast, the alternative to the dominant . . . paradigm is derived from the tradition of anthropological field studies. Using the techniques of open-ended interviewing and personal observation, the alternative paradigm relies on qualitative data, holistic analysis, and detailed description derived from close contact with the targets of study. The . . . natural science paradigm aims at prediction of social phenomena; the holistic-inductive, anthropological paradigm aims at understanding of social phenomena.[11]

The central question is, of course, whether evaluation research ought to represent itself through its methodology as a hard science after the manner of chemistry or physics or as something closer to research in the humanities or the social sciences. In educational research in general[12] and in evaluation research in particular,[13] there seems to be a trend toward selecting among a variety of methodologies, in part because neither the natural science, social science, nor humanities approach is necessarily the correct one.[14] As Patton puts the matter, "The debate and competition between paradigms is being replaced by a new paradigm—*a paradigm of choices*. The paradigm of choices recognizes that different methods are appropriate for different situations."[15]

IV. 2. *Changing Perceptions of Writing, Ever-changing Writing Programs*

The changes in assumptions about program evaluation that we have described reflect broad changes in higher education in the years following World War II. The extension of educational opportunities to persons who traditionally had not attended college changed higher education from an essentially elitist to a fundamentally egalitarian institution. Most affected by these dramatic changes were programs teaching basic skills, especially introductory mathematics and writing programs. College and universities were simply not prepared to instruct the different kinds of students that appeared in large numbers on their campuses.

The changing student populations brought established methods of teaching writing into question. In 1961, Kitzhaber described two predominant ways of teaching writing—the literature approach and the rhetorical approach.[16] By the end of the 1950s, these approaches to the teaching of writing were recognized by some faculty members as inadequate. In 1959, Warner Rice called for English departments to stop teaching what they did not know how to teach and to return to the teaching of literature.[17] Further changes in American society during the 1960s accelerated the decline of the traditional approaches. The decade of the 1960s was the decade of liberal ideals: authority was challenged, requirements were dropped, and the written word was no longer sacrosanct. As Brent recollects:

> Students were turning in collages instead of essays in many composition courses. In one course in American literature taught by a teaching-assistant office-mate of mine, the students didn't write papers at all. They baked bread. Evidently, somewhere along the line, Thoreau produced a recipe for bread, and the students baked accordingly. They would line up outside the office with their loaves and approach my friend's desk where he had a paper plate and a big knife. He could cut a hunk off each loaf, chew it for fifteen seconds or so, progressively more slowly and slowly as his expression became more and more sagacious, and finally he would look at the student and say, "B plus" or "A minus."[18]

Ironically, the same liberal ideals that led in some places to the abolishment of freshman English as a required course eventually led to the reintroduction of writing into the college curriculum in a much more substantial way than ever before. College and universities nationwide relaxed their entrance requirements or made provisions for special admissions, giving access to higher education to a large segment of the population that previously had not attended college. The problem was not confined to institutions with open-admissions policies. Established universities, such as the University of California at Berkeley, found that a majority of students from middle-class backgrounds could not write "college-level" prose.

During the 1960s, another major change occurred in the social context that will likely alter substantially the nature of writing programs. This change was not obvious to us until we conducted a stratified survey of the writing of college-trained people in the work force.[19]

Although a great deal of anecdotal evidence has been collected that indicates writing is an important skill on the job, and several specialized surveys of writing in business and industry have been conducted, no one to our knowledge had attempted to survey a cross section of college graduates. We obtained a sample of 200 individuals which adequately fit the U.S. Department of Labor statistics on the distribution of college-educated people in the American work force. Over three-fourths of these college-trained people are employed in technical, professional, and managerial occupations, and fully half of all college-educated people are in technical and professional occupations. For all respondents the average total work time spent writing was 23.1 percent, or over one day in a five-day week. Nearly three-fourths of the people sampled claimed to spend 10 percent or more of their work time writing. Only four people claimed never to write while on the job. All of the people in technical and professional occupations wrote on the job, spending on the average 29 percent of total work time writing—a figure higher than for any other occupational group. What we found out about writing on the job runs directly counter to the views of many in academe about the importance of writing after college, a view still articulated by both faculty and students and accepted as fact by the Commission on English in 1966.[20] Writing *is* an important and frequently used skill across all major categories of occupations that college graduates are trained to enter. We are suggesting that it was not coincidental that the literacy crisis occurred at a time when many colleges and universities were reducing or abolishing their writing programs while the jobs that their graduates obtained required both more writing and more complex and diverse kinds of writing.

From the perspective of the early 1980s, we can see two major developments stemming from the inadequacy of the traditional approaches to the teaching of writing and the public outcry over the "literacy crisis." Both developments are related, and both are founded upon relationships between writing and thought. The more general development is the growing emphasis on processes in writing; the more specific development is the writing-across-the-curriculum movement,[21] a development which seems to have resulted as much from pressure brought to bear on English departments from the outside as from any measurable commitment to the concept from inside English departments. Among the more visible manifestations of these two developments have been the following:

1. Writing is no longer taught only in the English department or only in the freshman year.

2. Writing courses are recognized to have special needs, especially special training for their instructors.

3. Students write different types of writing for different audiences and purposes instead of themes.

4. The instructor's role has changed from strictly that of an evaluator to that of a coach.

5. Writing is taught by having students write instead of by lecture or discussion of readings.

6. Writing is not defined as a static product.[22]

The movement toward teaching writing as a process goes beyond merely having students write multiple drafts. It reinterprets the function of writing in the overall curriculum. Writing becomes a way of discovery. Students write not only to report what they know but also to discover connections of which they were not previously aware. Students can evaluate their ideas when they write because the ideas become explicit. Moreover, writing forces students to become active learners of a subject, to participate in the vital discussions of a discipline.

As we have pointed out in our discussion of the quantitative model, the change in the nature of writing courses also called into question prevailing ways of evaluating writing programs. The British Schools Council recognized this inadequacy when it commissioned a study of the writing development of children in British schools, not on the basis of quantitative measures such as clause length but in terms of the functions of what they wrote.[23] The work of the Schools Council research team, James Britton and his University of London colleagues, came to the conclusion that the great majority of texts written by schoolchildren were lifeless efforts addressed to the teacher as examiner.[24] When the interests of writing teachers and researchers turn to questions of process and function, the measures developed for pretest-posttest evaluation become inappropriate. At the same time, the expert-opinion approach to evaluation can be of little help because it lacks the theoretical underpinnings necessary to address questions of process and function. Significantly, Britton and his colleagues had to develop a theory of discourse in order to make judgments about the functions of writing in British schools. The changes in the nature of program evaluation, in writing programs, and in research in writing underscore the need for developing alternative models for writing program evaluation.

IV. 3. *Questions for Evaluators*

Patton's notion of a "paradigm of choices" is a useful one because the complexity of writing programs, we believe, precludes the use of a single approach in evaluation. Approaches to evaluation are, in effect, models of evaluation, such as the model we extracted from the four evaluation studies reviewed in chapter 2. The number of specific approaches to evaluation found in the literature is large, although none specifically addresses the problems of writing program evaluation.[25] From the standpoint of the evaluator of writing programs, the emergence of a "paradigm of choices" is fortuitous. Such a paradigm may lead to a synthesis of world views which will allow much greater latitude in deciding which kinds of data can be validly used in writing program evaluations and much greater latitude in the interpretation of those data. This is not to say that a "paradigm of choices" reduces the number of questions about the validity of materials or procedures. To the contrary, such a paradigm increases exponentially that number. While a "paradigm of choices" increases the options available to the evaluator, it does not eliminate the essential and fundamental differences in world view that the choices represent.

Knowledge of and skill in using qualitative approaches may very well extend our vision of writing program evaluation beyond its present moorings in product-oriented, pretest-posttest definitions of program effectiveness to the contexts of programs and the processes of learning and composing, but at the same time it forces us to decide which aspects of context, which aspects of learning, and which aspects of composing are worth the considerable effort and cost demanded by close observation. But it is only through a pluralism of approaches that evaluators will probably ever be able to address the complex sets of interactions among the components of writing programs posited at the end of chapter 3 or will probably ever be able to become sensitive to the rapid ever-changing nature of the thing evaluated.

As college and university writing programs continue to change in response to society's demands for a literate populace and in response to an ever-growing body of knowledge about both the products and processes of writing, evaluators will have to address increasingly complex questions and issues, and they will have to develop perhaps equally complex evaluations and procedures to address such questions and issues. The interactions among the five components specified at the end of chapter 3 can serve as a heuristic for identifying some of these questions.

One category of questions focuses on the writing program itself. For example, the interaction among social context, institutional context, and program structure might produce a question such as "What is the status of the academic unit responsible for developmental or remedial instruction?" This question would take into account the attitude of the society at large toward the students in the program, the institutional commitment to the education of those students, and the organization of a writing program that distinguishes between developmental and nondevelopmental students. A question such as "How successful are graduates of a developmental writing program in subsequent courses and in the world of work?" would necessarily involve all five components.

A second category of questions focuses on evaluation. We will group these questions according to the four constituencies of writing programs identified in chapter 3: the society, the institution, the program including its teacher and administrators, and the student.

One set of questions concerns the effects of writing programs on society. These questions might include:

1. Does the writing program affect the value its students place on the written language once they leave college?

2. Does the writing program, through its students and graduates, make the public sensitive to abuses of language?

3. Does the writing program help make the public aware of different uses of languages for different purposes?

4. Does the writing program affect the social and economic status of its students and graduates?

5. Does the writing program send students into the world better able to adapt the processes and products of writing to novel situations?

6. Does the writing program foster the development of cognitive skills that have application beyond writing?

7. Does the writing program contribute substantially to the operation of a democratic society, a society which is predicated on the assumption of a literate populace?

8. Does the writing program produce students and graduates who write in order to make sense of their experiences as human beings?

A second set of questions might focus on the effects of a program on the institution which houses it. These questions might include:

1. Are students capable of writing intelligently and clearly about specialized topics in disciplines other than English?

2. Are improvements in writing ability lost after students leave the composition program?

3. How does the writing program influence admissions requirements at a particular institution?

4. Does a writing program affect the number of degrees awarded at a particular institution?

5. To what extent does the size of a writing program affect the number of other courses offered?

6. How does a writing program affect the makeup of the faculty at a particular institution?

7. To what extent does a writing program promote communication among faculty and students in different disciplines on the basis of a common interest in written language?

8. How does the attitude of the composition teacher toward the teaching of writing and toward students of writing contribute to the attitudes of students toward the written language in general?

Another set of questions might be directed to interactions of various kinds among the components of writing programs. Among these questions are:

1. How does a writing program affect the attitudes of teachers in the program?

2. How does a writing program affect the professional status of teachers in the program?

3. How does the use of a required syllabus affect what and how particular teachers teach?

4. How do the support services and equipment (such as typing and copying services and audiovisual equipment) affect how well a teacher can teach?

5. How does the classroom itself—its size, arrangement, etc.—affect how well a teacher can teach?

6. How does the personality of a writing program director affect a writing program?

7. How does the process of administrative decision making affect what teachers and students do in a writing class?

8. How does the uniformity or lack of uniformity influence what teachers and students do in a writing class?

9. How does the selection of text materials affect the nature of curriculum?

A fourth set of questions could focus on the effects of writing programs on students. Such questions might be:

1. Do the theoretical underpinnings of a curriculum affect what students learn?

2. Do differing methods of delivery affect what students learn?

3. Do students' attitudes toward writing change as a result of being in a writing course?

4. Do curriculum and instruction affect students' awareness of their own composing processes?

5. Does the amount of time spent writing affect how well a student learns to write?

6. Does what a student learns in a writing course affect performance in subsequent courses?

7. Does the sequence of curricular elements affect how well a student learns to write?

8. What effect does instruction in critical reading have on the development of writing abilities?

Such questions as these are not easy ones to answer. They probe the nature and effects of writing programs. They address a complex and variously defined process called "learning to write." Furthermore, they consider "learning to write" as a process that extends beyond the classroom, that writing has important functions for both individual learners and society at large.

In the face of such complexity, the impulse is to turn away, either leaving writing program evaluations to others or concluding that sound evaluations of writing programs are impossible to achieve. Neither alternative is acceptable to our profession. By attempting to answer such questions, we can better come to know what we do, how we do it, and why it is important. If answers are possible, they are obtainable only through a pluralistic approach to evaluation that acknowledges the history of writing and the teaching of writing, builds on theories of learning and language, and incorporates a variety of evaluation methodologies and procedures.

Notes
Bibliography

Notes

1. The State of the Art of Evaluating Writing Programs

1. See Ernest R. House's *Evaluating with Validity* (Beverly Hills and London: Sage, 1980); Michael Q. Patton, *Qualitative Evaluation Methods* (Beverly Hills and London: Sage, 1980); and W. James Popham, *Educational Evaluation* (Englewood Cliffs: Prentice-Hall, 1975).
2. See Walter R. Borg and Meredith Damien Gall, *Educational Research: An Introduction*, 3d ed. (New York and London: Longman, 1979); Arieh Lewy (ed.), *Handbook of Curriculum Evaluation* (Paris and New York: UNESCO and Longman, 1977); Leonard Rutman, *Evaluation Research Methods: A Basic Guide* (Beverly Hills and London: Sage, 1977); Robert E. Stake (ed.), *Curriculum Evaluation* (Chicago: Rand McNally, 1967), and Stake, *Evaluating Educational Programmes: The Need and the Response* (Washington, DC: OECD Publications Center, 1976); and Blaine R. Worthen and James R. Sanders (eds.), *Educational Evaluation: Theory and Practice* (Worthington, OH: Charles A. Jones, 1973).
3. See "Evaluating Instruction in Writing: Approaches and Instruments," *College Composition and Communication* 33 (May 1982): 213–29. In addition to Larson, the members of this important committee are Lucy Grigsby, Kris Gutierrez, Maxine Hairston, James Kulik, Elizabeth McPherson, Ellen Nold, and Harvey Weiner.
4. See, for example, Barbara Gross Davis, Michael Scriven, and Susan Thomas, *The Evaluation of Composition Instruction* (Inverness, CA: Edgepress, 1981).
5. This project is supported in part by a grant from the Fund for the Improvement of Postsecondary Education. Some of the work of this project is discussed below.

6. See, for example, Charles R. Cooper and Lee Odell, "Introduction," in *Research on Composing: Points of Departure*, ed. Charles Cooper and Lee Odell (Urbana: National Council of Teachers of English, 1978), pp. xi–xvii, and Nancy I. Sommers, "The Need for Theory in Composition Research," *College Composition and Communication* 31 (1979): 46–49. In addition, Odell, in "Teachers of Composition and Needed Research in Discourse Theory," *College Composition and Communication* 30 (1979): 39–45, argues that theories of discourse need to be validated through experimental research involving writers of different ages. When such validation is accomplished, then it is proper to look for and test pedagogical applications.

7. Richard Braddock, Richard Lloyd-Jones, and Lowell Schoer, *Research in Written Composition* (Champaign: National Council of Teachers of English, 1963).

8. D. Gordon Rohman and Albert O. Wlecke, *Pre-Writing: The Construction and Application of Models for Concept Formation in Writing*, U.S. Office of Education Cooperative Research Project no. 2174 (East Lansing: Michigan State Univ., 1964). See also Rohman's "Pre-Writing: The Stage of Discovery in the Writing Process," *College Composition and Communication* 16 (1965): 106–12.

9. Several writers have addressed one or both of these issues. Among them are four whose work appears in *Sentence Combining and the Teaching of Writing*, ed. Donald Daiker, Andrew Kerek, and Max Morenberg (Akron: L & S Books, 1979): John C. Mellon, "Issues in the Theory and Practice of Sentence Combining: A Twenty-Year Perspective," pp. 1–38; James L. Kinneavy, "Sentence Combining in a Comprehensive Language Framework," pp. 60–76; Harold E. Nugent, "The Role of Old and New Information in Sentence Combining," pp. 201–8; and Arthur L. Palacas, "Towards Teaching the Logic of Sentence Connection," pp. 192–200. See also Andrew Kerek, "The Combining Process," in *Selected Papers from the 1981 Texas Writing Research Conference*, ed. Maxine Hairston and Cynthia Selfe (Austin: Univ. of Texas, 1981), pp. 97–115; and Joseph M. Williams, "Defining Complexity," *College English* 40 (Jan. 1980): 595–609.

10. NAEP reports have been issued regularly since 1970. The most important NAEP documents pertaining to the third and latest national assessment of writing are *Writing Achievement, 1969–79: Results from the Third National Writing Assessment, Volume I—17-Year-Olds*, Report no. 10-W-01 (Denver: NAEP, 1980); *Writing Achievement, 1969–79: Results from the Third National Writing Assessment, Volume II—13-Year-Olds*, Report no. 10-W-02 (Denver: NAEP, 1980); and *Writing Achievement, 1969–79: Results from the Third National Writing Assessment*,

Volume III—9-Year-Olds, Report no. 10-W-03 (Denver: NAEP, 1980). For a review of the materials on reading and writing released in 1972 and 1973 and for an evaluation of the assessment itself, see John C. Mellon, *National Assessment and the Teaching of English* (Urbana: National Council of Teachers of English, 1975). Mellon also examines the NAEP's *Writing Mechanics: 1969–1974* in "Round Two of the National Assessment—Interpreting the Apparent Decline in Writing Ability: A Review," *Research in the Teaching of English* 10 (1976): 66–74. For a discussion of many of the critical issues involved in such large scale testing, see Michael Clark, "Contests and Contexts: Writing and Testing in School," *College English* 42 (1980): 217–27, and Paul Olson, *A View of Power: Four Essays on the National Assessment of Educational Progress* (Grand Forks: Univ. of North Dakota Study Group on Evaluation, 1976).

11. 8 Dec. 1975, p. 58.
12. Some evidence of these developments in college writing programs appears in Stephen P. Witte, Paul R. Meyer, Thomas P. Miller, and Lester Faigley, *A National Survey of College and University Writing Program Directors,* FIPSE Grant G008005896 Technical Report no. 2 (Austin: Writing Program Assessment Office, Univ. of Texas, 1981), ERIC Doc. no. ED 210 709. See also Lawrence Peters, "Writing Across the Curriculum: Across the U.S.," mimeograph of a report detailing the results of a national survey conducted by the National Network of Writing Across the Curriculum Programs, George Mason Univ., 1982.
13. According to Norman Morris, "An Historian's View of Examinations," in *Examinations and English Education,* ed. Stephen Wiseman (Manchester: Manchester Univ. Pr., 1961), pp. 1–43, the first use of writing in mass testing occurred in Boston in 1845. By 1897, a major report by J. M. Rice was published in which inferences were drawn about the effectiveness of school districts on the basis of tests of language skills.
14. WPA Board of Consultant Evaluators, "Writing Program Evaluation: An Outline for Self-Study," *Journal of the Council of Writing Program Evaluators,* 4 (Winter 1980): 23–28.
15. Don E. Gardner, "Five Evaluation Frameworks: Implications for Decision Making in Higher Education," *Journal of Higher Education* 48 (1977): 574; and House, *Evaluating with Validity,* p. 36.
16. The literature in this area is large, but see, for example, K. R. Hammond, C. J. Hursh, and F. J. Todd, "Analyzing the Components of Clinical Inference," *Psychological Review* 72 (1965): 215–24; P. Slovic, "Analyzing the Expert Judge: A Descriptive Study of a Stockbroker's Decision Processes," *Journal of Experimental Psychology* 78 (1968), monograph supplement, no. 3, pt. 2; and P. Slovic and S. C. Lichten-

stein, "Comparison of Bayesian and Regression Approaches to the Study of Information Processing in Judgment," *Organizational Behavior and Human Performance* 6 (1971): 649–744.

2. *The Quantitative Model of Writing Program Evaluation*

1. *The Effectiveness of College-Level Instruction in Freshman Composition*, Final Report, Project no. 2188 (Washington, DC: Office of Education, U.S. Department of Health, Education, and Welfare, 1969). A report devoted to the pilot phase of this study was issued by the same authors; see *Interim Report: The Effectiveness of College-Level Instruction in Freshman Composition*, Cooperative Research Project 2188 (Cedar Falls: State College of Iowa, 1966). A follow-up study using the data collected by Jewell, Cowley, and Rhum, plus additional data collected from University of Iowa students involved in the UNI study, was completed by Richard Braddock. See his *Evaluation of College-Level Instruction in Freshman Composition: Part II*, Cooperative Research Project no. S-260 (Iowa City: Univ. of Iowa, 1968).
2. For an explication of those ETS procedures, see Fred Godshalk, Frances Swineford, and William E. Coffman, *The Measurement of Writing Ability* (New York: College Entrance Examination Board, 1966).
3. Donald Wesling, John Conlisk, Sharon Evans, W. G. Hardison, Ralph Loveberg, Emory Tolberg, and Jane Watkins, *Evaluation of the Four College Writing Programs at UC San Diego* (San Diego: Univ. of California, 1978).
4. Moffett's statement, "Evaluation of the Writing Programs at the University of California San Diego," appears as Appendix II in the Wesling et al. report. Wesling and his colleagues take issue with a number of Moffett's recommendations and criticisms. For an outline of these issues, see Wesling et al., pp. 12–18.
5. On the matter of variables left uncontrolled during the evaluation, see Wesling et al., pp. 34–35.
6. See, for example, Godshalk, Swineford, and Coffman, *The Measurement of Writing Ability* and Charles R. Cooper, "Holistic Evaluation of Writing," in *Evaluating Writing: Measuring, Describing, Judging*, ed. Charles R. Cooper and Lee Odell (Urbana: National Council of Teachers of English, 1977), pp. 3–31, which provides good bibliographies of works dealing with the evaluation of student writing.
7. Donald Daiker, Andrew Kerek, and Max Morenberg, "Sentence Combining and Syntactic Maturity in Freshman English," *College Composition and Communication* 29 (1978): 36–41; Morenberg, Daiker, and

Kerek, "Sentence Combining at the College Level: An Experimental Study," *Research in the Teaching of English* 12 (1978): 245–56; and Kerek, Daiker, and Morenberg, "Sentence Combining and College Composition," *Perceptual and Motor Skills* 51 (1980): 1059–1167 (Monograph Supplement 1-V51). Several questions were raised about the study as it was reported in 1978 in *College Composition and Communication*, in *Research in the Teaching of English*, and at the Wyoming Conference on Freshman and Sophomore English [see, for example, Kinneavy, "Sentence Combining in a Comprehensive Language Framework"; Mellon, "Issues in the Theory and Practice of Sentence Combining"; and Witte, "Review of *Sentence Combining and the Teaching of Writing*," *College Composition and Communication* 31 (1980): 433–37]. Because *Sentence Combining and College Composition* addresses several of those questions, we assume that it represents the final report on the Miami study. The following review is based on their most recent published report.

8. True control groups—students offered no instruction in writing—are often difficult to obtain. Many institutions are committed to placing all freshmen in composition courses during their first semester in college. For example, Lester Faigley was denied a request to form a control group by asking selected students to postpone freshman English for one semester. (See "The Influence of Generative Rhetoric on the Syntactic Fluency and Writing Effectiveness of College Freshmen," *Research in the Teaching of English* 13 (1979): 197–206.)

9. *Sentence Combining and College Composition*, p. 1101. The experimental group used William Strong's, *Sentence Combining: A Composing Book* (New York: Random, 1973) as their only textbook.

10. The curriculum of the control sections, in fact, followed the organization of James McCrimmon's *Writing with a Purpose*, 6th ed. (Boston: Houghton, 1976). A reader was also used.

11. *Syntactic fluency* refers to the relative sophistication with which writers of different ages are able to reduce clausal structures to less than clause status and to embed those reductions in the sentences they write. The term, *syntactic fluency*, is frequently used interchangeably with two other terms, *syntactic complexity* and *syntactic maturity*. The phenomenon presumably referred to by these terms is frequently measured by such indices as mean t-unit length (a t-unit being an independent clause plus all of its subordinate elements), mean clause length, and mean number of clauses per t-unit. These measures derive from the work of Kellogg Hunt, much of which is summarized in his "Early Blooming and Late Blooming Syntactic Structures," in *Evaluating Writing: Describing, Measuring, Judging*, pp. 91–104. Lester Faigley,

in "Names in Search of a Concept: Maturity, Fluency, Complexity, and Growth in Written Syntax," *College Composition and Communication* 31 (1980): 291–300, argues that for students beyond high school, it is impossible to tell what aspects of language development these terms refer to.

12. Morenberg, Daiker, and Kerek, "Sentence Combining at the College Level," pp. 253–55.

13. Ellen W. Nold and Sarah W. Freedman, "An Analysis of Readers' Responses to Essays," *Research in the Teaching of English* 11 (1977): 164–74; Faigley, "The Influence of Generative Rhetoric."

14. See, for example, Mellon, "Issues in the Theory and Practice of Sentence Combining," pp. 26–34; Kinneavy, "Sentence Combining in a Comprehensive Language Framework," pp. 66–67; and Witte, "Review of *Sentence Combining and the Teaching of Writing*."

15. *Transformational Sentence Combining: A Method for Enhancing Syntactic Fluency in English Composition*, Research Report no. 10 (Champaign: National Council of Teachers of English, 1969).

16. *Sentence Combining: Improving Student Writing Without Formal Grammar Instruction*, Research Report no. 15 (Champaign: National Council of Teachers of English, 1973).

17. Daiker, Kerek, and Morenberg, "Using 'Open' Sentence-Combining Exercises in the College Composition Classroom," in *Sentence Combining and the Teaching of Writing*, p. 168.

18. Many of the rhetorical principles were obviously drawn from the work of Francis Christensen, as evidenced in Strong's *Sentence Combining: A Composing Book*. The North Dakota study of generative rhetoric—which was designed, in part, as a replication of the Miami study—yielded similar results in both syntactic features and holistic scores (Faigley, "The Influence of Generative Rhetoric"). Although the North Dakota study has many of the same weaknesses as the Miami study, the rhetorical assumptions were made more deliberately a part of a curriculum, primarily because the Christensen materials make many of these rhetorical assumptions explicit.

19. On these matters, see the investigators' comparisons of the two courses, pp. 1090–1103.

20. Stephen P. Witte and Lester Faigley, *A Comparison of Analytic and Synthetic Approaches to the Teaching of College Writing*, TWRG Research Report no. 1 (Austin: Department of English, Univ. of Texas, 1981), ERIC Doc. no. ED 209 677.

21. *A Theory of Discourse* (1971; reprint, New York: Norton, 1980).

22. These purposes and modes of discourse were presented through a course

syllabus supplemented, when available, by parallel treatments from Michael E. Adelstein and Jean Pival's *The Writing Commitment* (New York: Harcourt, 1976) and by exemplary readings from Randall E. Decker's (ed.) *Patterns in Exposition 6* (Boston: Little, 1978). For instruction in the conventions of standard written English, students relied on Jim W. Corder's *Handbook of Current English* (Glenview, IL: Scott, Foresman, 1978).

23. "A Conceptual Rhetoric of the Composition," *College Composition and Communication* 22 (1971): 348–54.

24. Susan W. Wittig, *Steps to Structure* (Cambridge, MA: Winthrop, 1975).

25. Because the text materials for the meristic option relied on considerable grammatical terminology, teachers employing this approach used J. C. Blumenthal's *English 3200: A Programmed Course in Grammar and Usage* (New York: Harcourt, 1972), a programmed grammar text to teach students grammatical vocabulary and to teach them conventional usage. As part of the second option's curriculum, *English 3200* was intended to provide students with the competencies that would enable them to complete the more sophisticated sentence-level exercises available interactively by computer. See Susan W. Wittig, *Dialogue* (Iowa City: Conduit, 1978), and "Dialogue: Project C-BE Drill and Practice," *Pipeline* 4 (1978): 20–22. These exercises, in turn, prepared students to handle the treatments of paragraphs and essays in Wittig's *Steps to Structure*.

26. The research design as well as the comparisons are presented in detail in Witte and Faigley, *A Comparison of Analytic and Synthetic Approaches*, pp. 7–10, 295–300.

27. John A. Daly and Michael D. Miller, "The Empirical Development of an Instrument to Measure Writing Apprehension," *Research in the Teaching of English* 9 (1975): 242–49.

28. A. L. Raygor, *McGraw-Hill Basic Skills System Reading Test: Examiner's Manual* (New York: McGraw-Hill, 1970).

29. A. L. Raygor, *McGraw-Hill Basic Skills System Writing Test: Examiner's Manual* (New York: McGraw-Hill, 1970). For the two McGraw-Hill tests, Forms A and B were used, with one class on each side of each principal comparison receiving Form A as a pretest and one class on each side of each principal comparison receiving Form B. For the posttest the forms were reversed for each section.

30. The topics are reproduced in Witte and Faigley, *A Comparison of Analytic and Synthetic Approaches*, pp. 13–16. Posttest data were collected during the last week of classes and during the final examination period. Because the essays the students wrote were used in computing course

grades, they were photocopied for holistic scoring prior to their having been marked by the teachers for return to the students. Students were given extra credit for completing the two McGraw-Hill tests.

31. Interrater reliabilities for the two narrative-descriptive essays were computed to be .76 and .78, respectively; and for the two argumentative essays, they were computed to be .82 and .84, respectively. The *McGraw-Hill Reading Test* and *Writing Test* and the Miller-Daly WAT were computer scored. Data from each comparison were submitted to analyses of covariance, with pretest scores used as covariates to control for pretest differences.

32. See Witte and Faigley, *A Comparison of Analytic and Synthetic Approaches*, pp. 127–242.

33. These analyses are presented in Witte and Faigley, *A Comparison of Analytic and Synthetic Approaches*, pp. 243–49. See also Faigley, Daly, and Witte, "The Role of Writing Apprehension in Writing Performance and Competence," *Journal of Educational Research* 75 (Sept.–Oct. 1981): 16–21.

34. Type 2 errors occur when statistical power is inadequate to accept the null hypothesis. Statistical power in the Texas study was low owing to the small number of subjects in each call. B. J. Winer suggests that .30 and .20 levels of significance may be more appropriate under these conditions than .05 and .01. See *Statistical Principles in Experimental Design*, 2d ed. (New York: McGraw-Hill, 1971), p. 14.

35. On this point see Lee Odell's discussion in "Defining and Assessing Competence in Writing," in *The Nature and Measurement of Competency in English*, ed. Charles R. Cooper (Urbana: National Council of Teachers of English, 1981), pp. 107–8; Gabriel Della-Piana, Lee Odell, Charles Cooper, and George Endo, "The Writing Skills Decline: So What?" in *The Test Score Decline: Meaning and Issues*, ed. Lawrence Lipsitz (Englewood Cliffs: Educational Technology Publications, 1977), pp. 163–86.

36. J. C. Seegars, "The Form of Discourse and Sentence Structure," *Elementary English* 10 (1933): 51–54; Lois V. Johnson, "Children's Writing in Three Forms of Composition," *Elementary English* 44 (1967): 265–69; L. Ramon Veal and Murray Tillman, "Mode of Discourse Variation in the Evaluation of Children's Writing," *Research in the Teaching of English* 5 (1971): 37–45; Marion Crowhurst and Gene L. Piche, "Audience and Mode of Discourse Effects on Syntactic Complexity in Writing at Two Grade Levels," *Research in the Teaching of English* 13 (1979): 101–9; Faigley, "Names in Search of a Concept."

37. As far as we know, composition researchers have always treated holistic scores as though they represented a continuous variable, like age or

weight. However, holistic evaluation involves placing essays into categories or groups according to their relative quality. Unlike a variable such as age, a holistic score can be no higher than the number assigned to that particular category of essays, the numerical "value" of the essay representing simply a name for a category. It may be argued that it makes no more sense to treat a holistic score as though it were a numerical value than it does to assign a number name to sex or race and then treat the data as numerical. What would it mean if we were to say that a given population had an average racial makeup of 4.85? Perhaps holistic scores should be treated as categorical rather than numerical data. This is, however, a topic far too technical for full treatment here, although it is one to which researchers should address themselves. The issue, of course, has a number of implications not only for the evaluation of writing courses and programs but for writing research in general and for the work of the Educational Testing Service in particular.

38. Sarah W. Freedman, "Influences on Evaluators of Expository Essays: Beyond the Text," *Research in the Teaching of English* 15 (1981): 245–55; and Freedman and Robert Calfee, "Holistic Assessment of Writing: Experimental Design and Cognitive Theory" (unpublished MS).

3. A Framework for Evaluating College Writing Programs

1. Ralph W. Tyler, *Basic Principles of Curriculum and Instruction* (Chicago: Univ. of Chicago Pr., 1950); and "The Functions of Measurement in Improving Instruction," in *Educational Measurement*, ed. E. F. Linquist (Washington, DC: American Council on Education, 1951), pp. 47–67.

2. On this matter, see Arieh Lewy, "The Nature of Curriculum Evaluation," in *Handbook of Curriculum Evaluation*, ed. Arieh Lewy (Paris and New York: UNESCO and Longman, 1977), pp. 10–11. Tyler's model has been criticized by Robert E. Stake, "Language, Rationality and Assessment," in *Improving Educational Assessment*, ed. W. H. Beatty (Washington, DC: Association for Supervision and Curriculum Development, 1969), pp. 14–40, for not adequately accommodating process variables or the conditions which give rise to products. The Tyler model has also been criticized for similar reasons by Michael Scriven, "The Methodology of Evaluation," in *Perspectives on Curriculum Evaluation*, ed. Ralph W. Tyler (Chicago: Rand McNally, 1967), pp. 39–83; and by G. V. Glass, *The Growth of Evaluation Methodology* (Boulder: Laboratory of Educational Research, Univ. of Colorado, 1969).

3. On this matter, see House, *Evaluating with Validity*, p. 27.

4. See Stephen P. Witte, Roger D. Cherry, and Paul R. Meyer, *The Goals of Freshman Writing Programs as Perceived by a National Sample of College and University Writing Program Directors and Teachers*, FIPSE Grant G008005896, Technical Report no. 5 (Austin: Writing Program Assessment Office, Univ. of Texas, 1982). ERIC Doc. no. ED 216 395.

5. See, for example, Jack Goody, *Domestication of the Savage Mind* (Cambridge: Cambridge Univ. Pr., 1977); *Literacy in Traditional Societies* (Cambridge: Cambridge Univ. Pr., 1969): Eric A. Havelock, *Origins of Western Literacy* (Toronto: Ontario Institute for Studies in Education, 1976).

6. See Richard Ohmann, *English in America* (New York: Oxford Univ. Pr., 1976); and Shirley Brice Heath, "The Functions and Uses of Literacy," *Journal of Communication*, 30 (1980): 123–33.

7. Heath, "Toward an Ethnohistory of Writing in American Education," in *Writing: The Nature, Development, and Teaching of Written Communication; Volume 1, Variation in Writing: Functional and Linguistic-Cultural Differences*, ed. Marcia Farr Whiteman (Hillsdale, NJ: Lawrence Erlbaum, 1981), pp. 25–45.

8. Lester Faigley, Thomas P. Miller, Paul R. Meyer, and Stephen P. Witte, *Writing after College: A Stratified Survey of the Writing of College-Trained People*, FIPSE Grant G008005896, Technical Report no. 1 (Austin: Writing Program Assessment Office, Univ. of Texas, 1981). ERIC Doc. no. ED 210 708.

9. T. Neville Postlethwaite, "Determination of General Educational Aims and Objectives," in *Handbook of Curriculum Evaluation*, esp. pp. 56–60. Postlethwaite's source is F. B. Womer, *What Is National Assessment?* (Ann Arbor: National Assessment of Educational Progress, 1970).

10. In fact, the Comptroller General's Report to the Congress, *The National Assessment of Educational Progress: Its Results Need to Be Made More Useful* (Washington, DC: U.S. General Accounting Office, 1976) criticized the first assessments for NAEP's failure to take into account the students' varying backgrounds.

11. See Roy D. Goldman and David J. Hudson, "A Multivariate Analysis of Academic Abilities and Strategies for Successful and Unsuccessful College Students in Different Major Fields," *Journal of Educational Psychology* 65 (1973): 364–70; and Roy D. Goldman and Rebecca Warren, "Discriminant Analysis of Study Strategies Connected with Grade Success in Different Major Fields," *Journal of Educational Measurement* 10 (1973): 39–47.

12. Carl Frederiksen, "Abilities, Transfer and Information Retrieval in Verbal Learning," *Multivariate Behavior Research Monographs* 2 (1969): 1–82.

13. R. Havinghurst, *Developmental Tasks and Education*, 3d ed. (New York: David McKay, 1973).

14. There is a considerable literature available on the subject of contextual influences on educational programs. See, for example, Raymond S. Adams, Richard M. Kimble, and Marjorie Martin, "School Size, Organizational Structure and Teaching Practices," *Educational Administration Quarterly* 6 (Autumn 1970): 15–31; Egon G. Guba and Charles E. Bidwell, *Administrative Relationships: Teacher Effectiveness, Teacher Satisfaction and Administrative Behaviour* (Chicago: Midwest Administration Centre, Univ. of Chicago, 1957); and Ralph W. Larkin, "Contextual Influences on Teacher Leadership Styles," *Sociology of Education* 46 (1973): 471–79. Jacque Barzun in his 1960s treatise on the American university, discusses many political and social influences of context on higher education in this country. See his *The American University: How It Runs, Where It is Going* (New York: Harper, 1968).

15. "Diving In: An Introduction to Basic Writing," *College Composition and Communication* 27 (1976): 234–39; *Errors and Expectations: A Guide for the Teacher of Basic Writing* (New York: Oxford Univ. Pr., 1977). See also Shaughnessy's review of research in basic writing: "Basic Writing," in *Teaching Composition: 10 Bibliographical Essays*, ed. Gary Tate (Fort Worth: Texas Christian Univ. Pr., 1976), pp. 137–67.

16. Many writers might be cited here. Among those are several of the essayists represented in two recent collections: Walker Gibson (ed.) *New Students in Two-Year Colleges: Twelve Essays* (Urbana: National Council of Teachers of English, 1979) and Lawrence N. Kasden and Daniel R. Hoeber (eds.) *Basic Writing: Essays for Teachers, Researchers, and Administrators* (Urbana: National Council of Teachers of English, 1980). On some of the specific needs of basic writers, Andrea A. Lunsford's "Cognitive Development and the Basic Writer," *College English* 41 (Sept. 1979): 39–46, is an especially important essay. Also relevant is Muriel Harris's "Individualized Diagnosis: Teaching for Causes, Not Symptoms, of Writing Deficiencies," *College English* 40 (Nov. 1978): 318–33, and Harvey S. Wiener's "Basic Writing: First Day's Thoughts on Process and Detail," in *Eight Approaches to Teaching Composition*, ed. Timothy R. Donovan and Ben W. McClelland (Urbana: National Council of Teachers of English, 1981), pp. 87–99.

17. Leonard Rutman, *Planning Useful Evaluations: Evaluability Assessment*, with a "Forward" by Joseph S. Wholey (Berkeley and London: Sage, 1980), esp. pp. 89–104.

18. See Witte, Meyer, Miller, and Faigley, *A National Survey of College and University Writing Program Directors*, pp. 104–5.

19. For discussions by various hands of the "writing across the curriculum" movement, see Toby Fulwiler and Art Young (eds.), *Language Connections: Writing and Reading Across the Curriculum* (Urbana: National Council of Teachers of English, 1982). See also Peters, "Writing Across the Curriculum."

20. A fair amount of this research is summarized in Eric Bredo, "Contextual Influences on Teachers' Instructional Approaches," *Journal of Curriculum Studies* 12 (1980): 49–60.

21. See Witte, Meyer, Miller, and Faigley, *A National Survey of College and University Writing Program Directors*, esp. pp. 112–16.

22. Gilbert Ryle, *The Concept of Mind* (New York: Barnes, 1949), pp. 59–60.

23. Considerable evidence of both kinds of curricular variables is presented in Stephen P. Witte and Paul R. Meyer with Thomas P. Miller, *A National Survey of College and University Teachers of Writing*, FIPSE Grant G008005896, Technical Report no. 4 (Austin: Writing Program Assessment Office, Univ. of Texas, 1982). ERIC Doc. no. ED 219 779.

24. See Richard E. Young, "Paradigms and Problems: Needed Research in Rhetorical Invention," in *Research on Composing: Points of Departure*, pp. 29–47; James A. Berlin and Robert P. Inkster, "Current-Traditional Rhetoric: Paradigm and Practice," *Freshman English News* 8, no. 3 (Winter 1980): 1–4, 13–14; Donald C. Stewart, "Composition Textbooks and the Assault on Tradition," *College Composition and Communication* 29 (1978): 171–76; and Maxine Hairston, "The Winds of Change: Thomas Kuhn and Revolution in the Teaching of Writing," *College Composition and Communication* 33 (1982): 76–88. We might speculate that the traditional paradigm is not likely to change either substantially or quickly unless and until composition teachers accord textbooks considerably less status than they presently have in the teaching of writing. Textbooks, to be sure, are useful for teaching content in the sense of *what*, but they are of considerably less value in teaching content in the sense of *how*. The reason for this, of course, is that they can only address *how* by converting it to *what*. On this latter issue, see also Mike Rose, "Sophisticated, Ineffective Books—The Dismantling of Process in Composition Texts," *College Composition and Communication* 32 (1981): 65–74.

25. Witte, Meyer, Miller, and Faigley, *A National Survey of College and University Writing Program Directors*, pp. 57–65.

26. "Composition Textbooks and Pedagogical Theory: A Review-Essay," *College English* 43 (1981): 393–409.

27. Woods acknowledges his debt to Barry Kroll, "Developmental Perspec-

tives and the Teaching of Composition," *College English* 41 (1980): 741–52, for this term.

28. Stephen Judy's "The Experimental Approach: Inner Worlds to Outer Worlds," in *Eight Approaches to Teaching Composition*, ed. Timothy R. Donovan and Ben W. McClelland (Urbana: National Council of Teachers of English, 1981), pp. 37–51, provides what we think is a good account of the "expressionist" approach Woods describes.

29. "The Search for Intelligible Structure in the Teaching of Composition," *College Composition and Communication* 27 (1976): 142–47. A somewhat less ambitious, but nonetheless valuable, delineation of an underlying structure for teaching composition is found in Caroline D. Eckhardt and Donald C. Stewart, "Toward a Functional Taxonomy of Composition," *College Composition and Communication* 30 (1979): 338–42. Eckhardt and Stewart distinguish between two approaches to composition, one through *techniques* and one through *purposes*. This is essentially a distinction between *how* and *why*, between *means* and *ends*, between *modes* and *aims*. This distinction is built into D'Angelo's structure, but Eckhardt and Stewart stress the primacy of *purposes* and offer a taxonomy of purposes which differs in important ways from the one built into D'Angelo's structure.

30. *English Composition and Rhetoric*, rev. American ed. (New York: D. Appleton, 1890).

31. *A Theory of Discourse*. For less thorough treatments, see his "Basic Aims of Discourse," *College Composition and Communication* 20 (1969): 297–313, and his collaborative work with John Q. Cope and J. W. Campbell, *Aims and Audiences* (Dubuque: Kendall/Hunt, 1976). Kinneavy's theory of discourse modes is set down in another collaborative work with Cope and Campbell, *Writing—Basic Modes of Organization* (Dubuque: Kendall/Hunt, 1976). Richard H. Haswell, "Tactics of Discourse: A Classification for Student Writers," *College English* 43 (Feb. 1981): 168–78, raises a number of objections on pedagogical grounds to Kinneavy's theory of aims and modes. Lee Odell, "Teachers of Composition and Needed Research in Discourse Theory," questions the basis of Kinneavy's claim that aim or purpose is all important.

32. See *Teaching the Universe of Discourse* (Boston: Houghton, 1968); "A Structural Curriculum in English," *Harvard Educational Review* 36 (1966): 17–28; and "A Rationale for a New Curriculum in English," in *Rhetoric: Theories for Application*, ed. Robert M. Gorrell (Champaign: National Council of Teachers of English, 1967), pp. 114–21.

33. See Britton, Burgess, Martin, McLeod, and Rosen, *The Development of Writing Abilities (11–18)* (London: Macmillan Education Ltd, 1975);

and Britton, "The Composing Processes and the Functions of Writing," in *Research on Composing: Points of Departure*, pp. 13–28.

34. See J. A. van Ek with contributions by L. G. Alexander, *The Threshold Level for Modern Language Learning in Schools* (London: Longman, 1976).

35. "Theories of Composition and Actual Writing," *Kansas English* 59 (Dec. 1973): 3–17; for a more recent statement, together with a greater historical treatment, see Kinneavy's "Translating Theory into Practice in Teaching Composition: A Historical and a Contemporary View," in *Classical Rhetoric in Modern Discourse*, ed. Robert J. Connors, Lisa Ede, and Andrea Lunsford (Carbondale: Southern Illinois Univ. Pr., *in press*).

36. The best modern representative of this approach is Edward P. J. Corbett, *Classical Rhetoric for the Modern Student* (New York: Oxford Univ. Pr., 1971); and "A New Look at Old Rhetoric," in *Rhetoric: Theories for Application*, pp. 16–22. See also John H. Macklin, *Classical Rhetoric for Modern Discourse: An Art of Invention, Arrangement, and Style for Readers, Speakers, and Writers* (New York: Free Pr., 1969).

37. According to Kinneavy, the best modern exemplar of this approach is Francis Christensen, *The Christensen Rhetoric Program* (New York: Harper, 1968).

38. See Ken Macrorie, *Telling Writing* (Rochelle Park, NJ: Hayden, 1970) and *Writing to Be Read* (Rochelle Park, NJ: Hayden, 1968).

39. See Carl H. Klaus, *Style in English Prose* (New York: Macmillan, 1969), and Gerald Levin (ed.), *Prose Models* (New York: Harcourt, 1975).

40. See Robert Zoellner, "Talk-Write: A Behavioral Pedagogy for Composition," *College English* 30 (1969); 267–320. For part of the debate which ensued from Zoellner's essay, see "On Zoellnerism," *College English* 30 (1969): 645–68, which contains a number of responses by various hands to Zoellner's behavioral approach.

41. See Peter Elbow, *Writing Without Teachers* (London: Oxford Univ. Pr., 1973), and *Writing with Power: Techniques for Mastering the Writing Process* (Oxford: Oxford Univ. Pr., 1981) and "A Method for Teaching Writing," *College English* 30 (1968): 115–25. William J. Coles, Jr., and his disciples should also be included within this class. See Coles, "The Teaching of Writing as Writing," *College English* 29 (1967): 111–16, and *The Plural I: The Teaching of Writing* (New York: Holt, 1978), as well as Kenneth Dowst, "The Epistemic Approach: Writing, Knowing, and Learning," in *Eight Approaches to Teaching Composition*, pp. 37–51. Also a champion of the "Learning by Doing" method is James Moffett, *Teaching the Universe of Discourse*, esp. chap. 6, pp. 188–210.

42. See *Notes Toward a New Rhetoric: Six Essays for Teachers* (New York:

Harper, 1968). Some of the curricular and instructional variables involved in generative rhetoric are discussed in Norton Kinghorn, Lester Faigley, and Thomas Clemens, *A Syntactic Approach to College Writing: An Analysis of Theory and Effect* (Grand Forks: Univ. of North Dakota Study Group on Evaluation, 1981).

43. For illustration, see Francis Christensen, *The Christensen Rhetoric Program*; Bonniejean Christensen, *The Christensen Method* (New York: Harper, 1979); Francis and Bonniejean Christensen, *A New Rhetoric* (New York: Harper, 1976); and Susan Wittig, *Steps to Structure.*

44. Roger W. Shuy, "A Holistic View of Language," *Research in the Teaching of English* 15 (1981): 101–11.

45. For example, Andrea Lunsford, "Cognitive Development and the Basic Writer."

46. Bruce R. Joyce and M. Weil, *Models of Teaching* (Englewood Cliffs: Prentice-Hall, 1979). See also Joyce's summary statement, "A Problem of Categories: Classifying Approaches to Teaching," *Journal of Education* 160 (Aug. 1978): 67–95. Joyce contends that two problems, one linguistic and one conceptual affect discussions of teaching adversely. The first problem is that the term *teaching* is often used in an undifferentiated way, and the second is that scholarship on teaching is based on "value orientations which masquerade in analytic dress."

47. See, for example, the essays collected in P. L. Peterson and H. J. Walberg (eds.), *Research on Teaching* (Berkeley: McCutchan, 1979).

48. Elizabeth McPherson, "Composition," in *The Teaching of English, the 76th Yearbook of the National Society for the Study of Education*, pt. 1, ed. James R. Squire (Chicago: National Society for the Study of Education, 1977), pp. 178–88.

49. On this matter, see John Dixon, *Growth in English* (New York: Oxford Univ. Pr., 1967).

50. See Donald M. Murray, *A Writer Teaches Writing: A Practical Method of Teaching Composition* (Boston: Houghton, 1968); Thomas Carnicelli, "The Writing Conference: A One-to-One Conversation," in *Eight Approaches to Teaching Composition*, pp. 101–31. See also Charles R. Duke, "The Student Centered Conference and the Writing Process," *English Journal* 64 (Dec. 1975): 44–47.

51. For a definition of the conferencing method, a discussion of the assumptions underlying the approach, and a discussion of the teacher's role, see Carnicelli, "The Writing Conference: A One-to-One Conversation," pp. 102–19. Although the conferencing method has received a great deal of attention, knowledge of how and why it works remains largely anecdotal in nature. As far as we know, only one researcher—Sarah W. Freedman—is presently trying to extend knowledge beyond

the level of the anecdotal. See her "Evaluation in the Writing Conference: An Interactive Process," in *Selected Papers from the 1981 Texas Writing Research Conference*, pp. 65–96.

52. Roger Garrison, "One to One: Tutorial Instruction in Freshman Composition," in *New Directions for Community Colleges* (San Francisco: Jossey-Bass, 1974), pp. 55–83.

53. See Kenneth Bruffee, "The Brooklyn Plan: Attaining Intellectual Growth through Peer-Group Tutoring," *Liberal Education* 64 (1978): 447–68, and his "Collaborative Learning: Some Practical Models," *College English* 34 (1973): 634–43. For other treatments of collaborative learning and the use of peer groups, see Thom Hawkins, *Group-Inquiry Techniques for Teaching Writing* (Urbana: National Council of Teachers of English and the ERIC Clearinghouse on Reading and Communication Skills, 1976), and "Intimacy and Audience: The Relationship Between Revision and the Social Dimensions of Peer Tutoring," *College English* 42 (1980): 64–68; and Richard Gebhardt, "Teamwork and Feedback: Broadening the Base of Collaborative Writing," *College English* 42 (1980): 69–74. Also relevant are Neil Ellman, "Peer Evaluation and Peer Grading," *English Journal* 64 (Mar. 1975): 79–80; Allan A. Glutthorn, "Cooperate and Create: Teaching Writing Through Small Groups," *English Journal* 62 (Dec. 1973): 1274–75; and Theodore W. Hipple, "The Grader's Helpers—Colleagues, Peers, and Scorecards," *English Journal* 61 (May 1972): 690–93.

54. Witte, Meyer, and Miller, in *A National Survey of College and University Teachers of Writing*, report that the use of peer tutoring, conferencing, and collaborative learning were the instructional methods most often named as *the most successful aspects* of the teaching of a national sample of the *best* college and university writing teachers in the country.

55. There is available a body of literature on the observation and description of instruction. For example, see Arno Bellak, *The Language of the Classroom* (New York: Teachers College Pr., 1966); Gary D. Borich, D. Malitz, C. L. Kugle, and M. Pascone, "Convergent and Discriminant Validity of Five Classroom Observation Systems: Testing and Modeling," *Journal of Educational Psychology* 70 (1978): 119–27; W. W. Cooley and G. Leinhardt, "The Instructional Dimensions Study," *Educational Evaluation and Policy Analysis* 2 (1980): 7–25; M. J. Dunkin and B. J. Biddle, *The Study of Teaching* (New York: Holt, 1974); Ned A. Flanders, "Interaction Analysis in the Classroom: A Manual for Observers," in *Mirrors for Behavior*, eds. Anita Simon and E. Gil Boyer (Philadelphia: Research for Better Schools, 1967); John Withall, W. W. Lewis, and John M. Newell, "Classroom Communication Observational Cate-

gories," in *Mirrors for Behavior*, eds. Anita Simon and E. Gil Boyer (Philadelphia: Research for Better Schools, 1967); and several of the essays anthologized in Jason Millman (ed.), *Handbook of Teacher Evaluation* (Beverly Hills: Sage in cooperation with the National Council on Educational Measurement, 1981).

56. On such practices, see, for example, Joseph J. Comprone, "The Uses of Media in Teaching Composition," in *Teaching Composition: 10 Bibliographical Essays*, ed. Gary Tate (Fort Worth: Texas Christian Univ. Pr., 1976), pp. 169–95.

57. On this matter, see the review of Computer Assisted Instructional (CAI) programs in Hugh L. Burns's "Stimulating Rhetorical Invention Through Computer Assisted Instruction," (Ph.D. diss., Univ. of Texas at Austin, 1979). For an accessible account of Burns's use of CAI in teaching invention, see Hugh L. Burns and George H. Culp, "Stimulating Invention in English Composition Through Computer-Assisted Instruction," *Educational Technology* 20, no. 8 (Aug. 1980): 5–10. For an indication of how different media can be used to stimulate writing, see Harvey S. Wiener, "Media Composition: Preludes to Writing," *College English* 35 (1974): 566–74, and Joseph Comprone, "Using Painting, Photography and Film to Teach Narration," *College English* 35 (1973): 174–78. Also relevant is Don M. Wolfe's *Creative Ways to Teach English* (New York: Odyssey, 1966). If the speculations of Jim Bencivenga, "Electronic Editing as a Tool," *English Journal* 71 (Jan. 1982): 91–92, are ever implemented on a wide scale, evaluators will also have to deal with the effects of text processing equipment on writing.

58. For a comprehensive review of the relevant literature, see Lester Faigley and Anna Skinner, *Writers' Processes and Writers' Knowledge: A Review of Research*, FIPSE Grant G008005896, Technical Report no. 6 (Austin: Writing Program Assessment Office, Univ. of Texas, 1982).

59. Michael Scriven, "Goal Free Evaluation," in *School Evaluation*, ed. Ernest R. House (Berkeley: McCutchan, 1973); "The Pros and Cons about Goal Free Evaluation," *Education Comment* 3 (1972): 1–4.

60. *Evaluating with Validity*, p. 30.

61. "Goal Free Evaluation," p. 321.

62. "Evaluation Bias and Its Control," in *Evaluation Studies Review Annual*, vol. 1, ed. G. V. Glass (Beverly Hills: Sage, 1976). However, in Scriven's recent work on evaluating composition instruction, he does not advocate a goal-free approach to evaluation. In fact, Scriven's statements on goal-free evaluation are not even referenced in the bibliography. See Davis, Scriven, and Thomas, *The Evaluation of Composition Instruction*.

63. See Stephen P. Witte, Roger D. Cherry, and Paul R. Meyer, *The Goals*

of Freshman Writing Programs as Perceived by a National Sample of College and University Writing Program Directors and Teachers, FIPSE Grant G008005896, Technical Report no. 5 (Austin: Writing Program Assessment Office, Univ. of Texas, 1982), ERIC Doc. no. ED 216 395, esp. pp. 6–7.

64. See Witte, Cherry, and Meyer, *The Goals of Freshman Writing Programs*, p. 29.

65. Faigley, Miller, Meyer, and Witte, *Writing after College: A Stratified Survey of the Writing of College-Trained People*, pp. 32–34.

66. A. M. Weinberg, *Reflections on Big Science* (Cambridge, MA: M.I.T. Pr., 1967). The passage is quoted from Goran Liede, "Experts' Judgements as Evaluation Data," in *Handbook of Curriculum Evaluation*, p. 181.

67. W. A. Scott, "Reliability of Content Analysis: The Case of Nominal Scale Coding," *Public Opinion Quarterly* 19 (1955): 321–25.

68. A. Kaplan, A. L. Skogstad, and M. A. Girshick, "The Prediction of Social and Technological Events," *Public Opinion Quarterly* 14 (1950): 93–110; A. F. Rasp, "Delphi: A Strategy for Decision Implementation," *Educational Planning* 1 (1974): 42–47.

69. Benjamin S. Bloom, Max D. Engelhart, Edward J. Furst, Walker H. Hill, and David R. Krathwohl, *Taxonomy of Educational Objectives, Handbook I: Cognitive Domain* (New York: David McKay, 1956).

70. David R. Krathwohl, Benjamin S. Bloom, and Bertram B. Masia, *Taxonomy of Educational Objectives, Handbook II: Affective Domain* (New York: David McKay, 1956).

71. Anita Harrow, *A Taxonomy of the Psychomotor Domain* (New York: David McKay, 1972).

72. Such an assumption may, however, be an ill-founded one. Although many composition teachers scoff at the suggestion that the physical act of writing words on paper may give some composition students problems, there is some evidence that some developmental students have not developed that skill. See Shaughnessy, *Errors and Expectations*.

73. Chew Tow Yow, "Evaluation at the Planning Stage," in *Handbook of Curriculum Evaluation*, p. 65.

74. Robert Gagne, *The Conditions of Learning*, 2d ed. (New York: Holt, 1970).

75. Lev Semenovich Vygotsky, *Language and Thought*, ed. and trans. Eugenia Haufmann and Gertrude Vakar (Cambridge, MA: M.I.T. Pr., 1962), esp. pp. 59–69.

76. Jean Piaget, *Six Psychological Studies* (New York: Random, 1967); *Judgment and Reasoning in the Child* (London: Kegan Paul, 1928); and *The*

Language and Thought of the Child (New York: New American Library, 1978).

77. Noam Chomsky, *Aspects of the Theory of Syntax* (Cambridge, MA: M.I.T. Pr., 1965). Not all students of language accept this dichotomy. One of the sharpest critics of the competence-performance distinction is M. A. K. Halliday. See particularly chap. 2 of his *Language as a Social Semiotic: The Social Interpretation of Meaning* (Baltimore: Univ. Park Pr., 1978).

78. It needs to be pointed out that neither the NAEP nor ETS has ever conducted assessments without the advice of "composition experts." The list of advisors to NAEP and the College Entrance Examination Board, the parent organization of ETS, often reads like a "Who's Who in Composition" in American colleges and universities. The point is that while members of the profession frequently criticize these groups, much of their work reflects the advice given by discipline experts from across the country.

79. For a discussion of these issues, see Hunter M. Breland and Judith L. Gaynor, "A Comparison of Direct and Indirect Assessments of Writing Skills," *Journal of Educational Measurement* 16 (1979): 119–28.

80. See, for example, Lee Odell and Charles R. Cooper, "Procedures for Evaluating Writing: Assumptions and Needed Research," *College English* 42 (1980): 35–43; Odell, "Defining and Assessing Competence in Writing."

81. NAEP, *Writing Achievement, 1969–79: Results from the Third National Writing Assessment, Volume III—9-Year-Olds*, p. 21.

82. Evidence of how experienced writers compose appears in several essays by Linda Flower and John R. Hayes: "The Cognition of Discovery: Defining a Rhetorical Problem," *College Composition and Communication* 31 (1980): 21–32; "A Cognitive Process Theory of Writing," *College Composition and Communication* 32 (1981): 365–87; "The Pregnant Pause: An Inquiry into the Nature of Planning," *Research in the Teaching of English* 15 (1981): 229–44. See also, Nancy I. Sommers, "Revision Strategies of Student Writers and Experienced Adult Writers," *College Composition and Communication* 31 (1980): 378–88; and Lester Faigley and Stephen Witte, "Analyzing Revision," *College Composition and Communication* 32 (1981): 400–14.

83. Witte, Meyer, and Miller, *A National Survey of College and University Teachers of Writing*.

84. See John A. Daly and Michael D. Miller, "Further Studies in Writing Apprehension: SAT Scores, Success Expectations, Willingness to Take Advanced Courses, and Sex Differences," *Research in the Teaching of*

English 9 (1975): 250–56; Daly and Wayne Shamo, "Writing Apprehension and Occupational Choice," *Journal of Occupational Psychology* 49 (1976): 55–56; Daly and Shamo, "Academic Decisions as a Function of Writing Apprehension," *Research in the Teaching of English* 12 (1978): 119–26.

4. Accommodating Context and Change in Writing Program Evaluation

1. Edward Suchman, *Evaluative Research* (New York: Russell Sage Foundation, 1967), p. 143.
2. It seems to us that, for example, Richard Larson's CCCC Committee on Teaching and Its Evaluation in Composition was formed primarily in response to questions about the validity of the conclusions drawn from extant materials and procedures on evaluating composition instruction. For the committee's most recent statement, see "Evaluating Instruction in Composition: Approaches and Instruments." The CCCC Research Committee's interest in the present monograph represents a similar response.
3. See, for example, John Mann, "The Outcome of Evaluation Research," in *Evaluating Action Programs: Readings in Social Action and Education* (Boston: Allyn & Bacon, 1972), p. 176.
4. On the educational backgrounds of college and university teachers of writing, see Witte, Meyer, and Miller, *A National Survey of College and University Teachers of Writing.*
5. Eisner, "On the Difference Between Scientific and Artistic Approaches to Qualitative Research," *Educational Researcher* 10, no. 4 (Apr. 1981): 7. See also his "On the Use of Educational Connoisseurship and Criticism for Evaluating Classroom Life," *Teachers College Record* 78 (1977): 345–58, and his *Educational Imagination: On the Design and Evaluation of School Programs* (New York: Macmillan, 1979).
6. Donald T. Campbell and Julian C. Stanley, "Experimental and Quasi-Experimental Designs for Research in Teaching," in *Handbook of Research on Teaching*, ed. Nathaniel L. Gage (Chicago: Rand McNally, 1963), p. 177. This Campbell and Stanley article was later reprinted as a monograph, *Experimental and Quasi-Experimental Designs for Research* (Chicago: Rand McNally, 1966).
7. Peter H. Rossi and Sonia R. Wright, "Evaluation Research: An Assessment of Theory, Practice, and Politics," *Evaluation Quarterly* 1 (1977): 13.
8. See his "Qualitative Knowing in Action Research." Paper presented at

the Annual Meeting of the American Psychological Association, New Orleans, 1974.

9. Lee J. Cronbach, "Beyond the Two Disciplines of Scientific Psychology," *American Psychologist* 30 (1975): 116–27.

10. Stephen Kemmis, "Telling It Like It Is: The Problem of Making a Portrayal of an Education Program," in *Curriculum Handbook: Administration and Theory*, vol. 2, ed. Louis Rubin (Boston: Allyn & Bacon, 1977), p. 359.

11. Michael Quinn Patton, *Utilization-Focused Evaluation* (Beverly Hills: Sage, 1978), pp. 203–4, 207. The passage is quoted from Patton, *Qualitative Evaluation Methods*, p. 19.

12. See, for example, Lee S. Shulman, "Disciplines of Inquiry in Education: An Overview," *Educational Researcher* 10 (June/July, 1981): 5–12, 23, and Eisner, "On the Difference Between Scientific and Artistic Approaches to Qualitative Research."

13. See Cronbach, "Beyond the Two Disciplines of Scientific Psychology"; and Patton, *Qualitative Evaluation Methods*, pp. 19–20.

14. Patton, *Qualitative Evaluation Methods*, p. 207.

15. *Qualitative Evaluation Methods*, p. 20. The same position is also taken by David L. Smith and Barry J. Fraser in "Towards a Confluence of Quantitative and Qualitative Approaches to Curriculum Evaluation," *Journal of Curriculum Studies* 12 (1980): 367–70.

16. Albert R. Kitzhaber, *Themes, Theories, and Therapy: The Teaching of College Writing* (New York: McGraw-Hill, 1963).

17. "A Proposal for the Abolition of Freshman English, As It Is Now Commonly Taught, from the College Curriculum," *College English* 21 (Apr. 1960): 361–67. A similar proposal was offered earlier by Oscar Campbell, "The Failure of Freshman English," *English Journal* 28 (1939): 177–85. Rice's proposal was reiterated by Katherine Bullard, "Academic Boondoggle," *College English* 25 (Feb. 1964): 373–75; and even more recently by Frederick E. Beckett, *College Composition: The Course Where a Student Doesn't Learn to Write* (Bruce, MS: Calcon Pr., 1974).

18. Harvey Brent, "Review of *The Survival of the 60s: Critical Teaching*," *College English* 43 (Dec. 1981): 834.

19. Faigley, Miller, Meyer, and Witte, *Writing after College: A Stratified Survey of the Writing of College-Trained People*.

20. We quote directly from *Freedom and Discipline in English: Report of the Commission on English* (New York: College Entrance Examination Board, 1966), p. 81, a passage that exposes the commission's ignorance of the complexity and the frequency of writing after college:

Caught between the reluctance to expose himself and indifference to subjects on which he really does not have anything he wants very much to say, the student may reasonably be inclined to argue that composition is a waste of time. He can point out that, whatever they say to the contrary, men rise to the top in commerce and industry who express themselves almost entirely by spoken words or in the limited written language of a science or technology; that it is perfectly possible to achieve high places in political and even diplomatic life without writing anything more complicated than factual reports. . . . He is likely to know, moreover, that most prominent and busy men have "writers" who compose for them, and he may even consider the plagiarizing of printed matter or of another student's essay not much different from reading aloud in public as one's own what someone else has actually written. He knows certainly that the world's business in these days is done largely by telephones and tape recorders, in conversations and conferences, in dictated memorandums and directives.

21. Peters, "Writing Across the Curriculum," reports that 122 writing-across-the-curriculum programs have been identified in American colleges and universities.
22. Evidence for many of these developments appears in Witte, Meyer, Miller, and Faigley, *A National Survey of College and University Writing Program Directors* and in Witte, Meyer, and Miller, *A National Survey of College and University Teachers of Writing.*
23. *Schools Council Working Paper Number Three* (London: Her Majesty's Stationery Office, 1965). This report is discussed in Peters, "Writing Across the Curriculum."
24. *The Development of Writing Abilities (11–18).*
25. For overviews of different approaches, see, for example, Daniel I. Stufflebeam, W. J. Foley, W. J. Gephart, E. G. Guba, H. D. Hammond, and M. M. Provus, *Educational Evaluation and Decision-Making* (Itasca, IL: Peacock, 1971), esp. pp. 9–16; Worthen and Sanders, *Educational Evaluation: Theory and Practice*; Popham, *Educational Evaluation*; Paul H. Dressler, *Handbook of Academic Evaluation* (San Francisco: Jossey-Bass, 1976), pp. 1–5; Robert E. Stake, *Evaluating Educational Programmes: The Need and the Response*; Lewy, "The Nature of Curriculum Evaluation," pp. 10–14; Don E. Gardner, "Five Evaluation Frameworks: Implications for Decision Making in Higher Education," pp. 571–93; and House, *Evaluating with Validity*, pp. 21–43.

Bibliography

Adams, Raymond S., Richard M. Kimble, and Marjorie Martin. "School Size, Organizational Structure and Teaching Practices," *Educational Administration Quarterly* 6 (Autumn 1970): 15–31.

Adelstein, Michael E., and James Pival. *The Writing Commitment*. New York: Harcourt, 1976.

Bain, Alexander. *English Composition and Rhetoric*, rev. American ed. New York: D. Appleton, 1890.

Barzun, Jacque. *The American University: How It Runs, Where It is Going*. New York: Harper, 1968.

Beatty, W. H., ed. *Improving Educational Assessment*. Washington, DC: Association of Supervision and Curriculum Development, 1969.

Beckett, Frederick E. *College Composition: The Course Where a Student Doesn't Learn to Write*. Bruce, MS: Calcon Pr., 1974.

Bellak, Arno. *The Language of the Classroom*. New York: Teachers College Pr., 1966.

Bencivenga, Jim. "Electronic Editing as a Tool," *English Journal* 71 (Jan. 1982): 91–92.

Berlin, James A., and Robert P. Inkster. "Current-Traditional Rhetoric: Paradigm and Practice," *Freshman English News* 8, no. 3 (Winter 1980): 1–4.

Bloom, Benjamin S., Max D. Englehart, Edward J. Furst, Walker H. Hill, and David R. Krathwohl. *Taxonomy of Educational Objectives, Handbook I: Cognitive Domain*. New York: David McKay, 1956.

Blumenthal, J. C. *English 3200: A Programmed Course in Grammar and Usage*. New York: Harcourt, 1972.

Borg, Walter R., and Meredith Damien Gall. *Educational Research: An Introduction*, 3d ed. New York and London: Longman, 1979.

Borich, Gary D., D. Malitz, C. L. Kugle, and M. Pascone. "Convergent and Discriminant Validity of Five Classroom Observation Systems: Testing and Modeling," *Journal of Educational Psychology* 70 (1978): 119–27.

Braddock, Richard. *Evaluation of College-Level Instruction in Freshman Composition: Part II*, Cooperative Research Project no. S-260. Iowa City: Univ. of Iowa, 1968.

———, Richard Lloyd-Jones, and Lowell Schoer. *Research in Written Composition*. Champaign, IL: National Council of Teachers of English, 1963.

Bredo, Eric. "Contextual Influences on Teachers' Instructional Approaches," *Journal of Curriculum Studies* 12 (1980): 49–60.

Breland, Hunter M., and Judith L. Gaynor, "A Comparison of Direct and Indirect Assessments of Writing Skills," *Journal of Educational Measurement* 16 (1979): 119–28.

Brent, Harvey. "Review of *The Survival of the 60s: Critical Teaching*," *College English* 43 (Dec. 1981): 824–38.

Britton, James. "The Composing Processes and the Functions of Writing." In *Research on Composing: Points of Departure*, ed. by Charles R. Cooper and Lee Odell, pp. 13–28. Urbana: National Council of Teachers of English, 1978.

———, Tony Burgess, Nancy Martin, Alex McLeod, and Harold Rosen. *The Development of Writing Abilities (11–18)*. London: Macmillan Education Ltd, 1975.

Bruffee, Kenneth. "The Brooklyn Plan: Attaining Intellectual Growth Through Peer-Group Tutoring," *Liberal Education* 64 (1978): 447–68.

———. "Collaborative Learning: Some Practical Models," *College English* 34 (1973): 634–43.

Bullard, Katherine. "Academic Boondoggle," *College English* 25 (Feb. 1964): 373–75.

Burns, Hugh L. "Stimulating Rhetorical Invention Through Computer Assisted Instruction." Ph.D. diss., Univ. of Texas at Austin, 1979.

———, and George H. Culp. "Stimulating Invention in English Composition Through Computer-Assisted Instruction," *Educational Technology* 20, no. 8 (Aug. 1980): 5–10.

Campbell, Donald T. "Qualitative Knowing in Action Research." Paper presented at the Annual Meeting of the American Psychological Association, New Orleans, 1974.

————, and Julian C. Stanley. "Experimental and Quasi-Experimental Designs for Research in Teaching." In *Handbook of Research on Teaching*, ed. by Nathaniel L. Gage, pp. 171–246. Chicago: Rand McNally, 1963.

————. *Experimental and Quasi-Experimental Designs for Research*. Chicago: Rand McNally, 1966.

Campbell, Oscar. "The Failure of Freshman English," *English Journal* 28 (1939): 177–85.

Carnicelli, Thomas. "The Writing Conference: A One-to-One Conversation." In *Eight Approaches to Teaching Composition*, ed. by Timothy R. Donovan and Ben W. McClelland, pp. 101–31. Urbana: National Council of Teachers of English, 1981.

Chomsky, Noam. *Aspects of the Theory of Syntax*. Cambridge, MA: M.I.T. Pr., 1965.

Christensen, Bonniejean. *The Christensen Method*. New York: Harper, 1979.

Christensen, Francis. *The Christensen Rhetoric Program*. New York: Harper, 1968.

————. *Notes Toward a New Rhetoric: Six Essays for Teachers*. New York: Harper, 1968.

————, and Bonniejean Christensen. *A New Rhetoric*. New York: Harper, 1976.

Clark, Michael. "Contests and Contexts: Writing and Testing in School," *College English* 42 (1980): 217–27.

Coles, William J., Jr. *The Plural I: The Teaching of Writing*. New York: Holt, 1978.

————. "The Teaching of Writing as Writing," *College English* 29 (1967): 111–16.

Commission on English. *Freedom and Discipline in English: Report of the Commission on English*. New York: College Entrance Examination Board, 1966.

Comprone, Joseph J. "The Uses of Media in Teaching Composition." In *Teaching Composition: 10 Bibliographical Essays*, ed. by Gary Tate, pp. 169–95. Fort Worth: Texas Christian Univ. Pr., 1975.

————. "Using Painting, Photography and Film to Teach Narration," *College English* 35 (1973): 174–78.

Comptroller General of the United States. *The National Assessment of Educational Progress: Its Results Need to Be Made More Useful*. Washington, DC: U.S. General Accounting Office, 1976.

Cooley, W. W., and G. Leinhardt. "The Instructional Dimensions Study," *Educational Evaluation and Policy Analysis* 2 (1980): 7–25.

Cooper, Charles R. "Holistic Evaluation of Writing." In *Evaluating Writing: Describing, Measuring, Judging,* ed. by Charles R. Cooper and Lee Odell, pp. 3–31. Urbana: National Council of Teachers of English, 1977.

———, ed. *The Nature and Measurement of Competency in English.* Urbana: National Council of Teachers of English, 1981.

———, and Lee Odell. "Introduction." In *Research on Composing: Points of Departure,* ed. by Charles R. Cooper and Lee Odell, pp. xi–xvii. Urbana: National Council of Teachers of English, 1978.

———, eds. *Research on Composing: Points of Departure.* Urbana: National Council of Teachers of English, 1978.

Corbett, Edward P. J. *Classical Rhetoric for the Modern Student.* New York: Oxford Univ. Pr., 1971.

———. "A New Look at Old Rhetoric." In *Rhetoric: Theories for Application,* ed. by Robert M. Gorrell, pp. 16–22. Champaign: National Council of Teachers of English, 1967.

Corder, Jim W. *Handbook of Current English.* Glenview, IL: Scott, Foresman, 1978.

Cronbach, Lee J. "Beyond the Two Disciplines of Scientific Psychology," *American Psychologist* 30 (1975); 116–27.

Crowhurst, Marion, and Gene L. Piche. "Audience and Mode of Discourse Effects on Syntactic Complexity in Writing at Two Grade Levels," *Research in the Teaching of English* 13 (1979): 101–9.

Daiker, Donald, Andrew Kerek, and Max Morenberg. "Sentence Combining and Syntactic Maturity in Freshman English," *College Composition and Communication* 29 (1978): 39–41.

———. "Using 'Open' Sentence-Combining Exercises in the College Composition Classroom." In *Sentence Combining and the Teaching of Writing,* ed. by Donald Daiker, Andrew Kerek, and Max Morenberg, pp. 160–69. Akron: L & S Books, 1979.

———, eds. *Sentence Combining and the Teaching of Writing.* Akron: L & S Books, 1979.

Daly, John A., and Michael D. Miller. "The Empirical Development of an Instrument to Measure Writing Apprehension," *Research in the Teaching of English* 9 (1975): 242–49.

———. "Further Studies in Writing Apprehension: SAT Scores, Success Expectations, Willingness to Take Advanced Courses, and Sex Differences," *Research in the Teaching of English* 9 (1975): 250–56.

————, and Wayne Shamo. "Academic Decisions as a Function of Writing Apprehension," *Research in the Teaching of English* 12 (1978): 119–26.

————. "Writing Apprehension and Occupational Choice," *Journal of Occupational Psychology* 49 (1976): 55–56.

D'Angelo, Frank J. "The Search for Intelligible Structure in the Teaching of Composition," *College Composition and Communication* 27 (1976): 142–47.

Davis, Barbara Gross, Michael Scriven, and Susan Thomas. *The Evaluation of Composition Instruction.* Inverness, CA: Edgepress, 1981.

Decker, Randall E., ed. *Patterns in Exposition 6.* Boston: Little, 1978.

Della-Piana, Gabriel, Lee Odell, Charles Cooper, and George Endo. "The Writing Skills Decline: So What?" in *The Test Score Decline: Meaning and Issues*, ed. by Lawrence Lipsitz, pp. 163–86. Englewood Cliffs: Educational Technology Publications, 1977.

Dixon, John. *Growth in English.* New York: Oxford Univ. Pr., 1967.

Donovan, Timothy R., and Ben W. McClelland, eds. *Eight Approaches to Teaching Composition.* Urbana: National Council of Teachers of English, 1981.

Dowst, Kenneth. "The Epsitemic Approach: Writing, Knowing, and Learning." In *Eight Approaches to Teaching Composition*, ed. by Timothy R. Donovan and Ben W. McClelland, pp. 37–51. Urbana, IL: National Council of Teachers of English, 1981.

Dressler, Paul H. *Handbook of Academic Evaluation.* San Francisco: Jossey-Bass, 1976.

Duke, Charles R. "The Student Centered Conference and the Writing Process," *English Journal* 64 (Dec. 1975): 44–47.

Dunkin, M. J., and B. J. Biddle. *The Study of Teaching.* New York: Holt, 1974.

Eckhardt, Caroline D., and Donald C. Stewart. "Toward a Functional Taxonomy of Composition," *College Composition and Communication* 30 (1979): 338–42.

Eisner, Elliot. "On the Difference Between Scientific and Artistic Approaches to Qualitative Research," *Educational Researcher* 10, no. 4 (Apr. 1981): 5–9.

————. *The Educational Imagination: On the Design and Evaluation of School Programs.* New York: Macmillan, 1979.

————. "On the Use of Educational Connoisseurship and Criticism for Evaluating Classroom Life," *Teachers College Record* 78 (1977): 345–58.

Elbow, Peter. "A Method for Teaching Writing," *College English* 30 (1968): 115–25.

———. *Writing Without Teachers.* London: Oxford Univ. Pr., 1973.

———. *Writing with Power: Techniques for Mastering the Writing Process.* Oxford: Oxford Univ. Pr., 1981.

Ellman, Neil. "Peer Evaluation and Peer Grading," *English Journal* 64 (Mar. 1975): 79–80.

Faigley, Lester. "The Influence of Generative Rhetoric on the Syntactic Fluency and Writing Effectiveness of College Freshmen," *Research in the Teaching of English* 13 (1979): 197–206.

———. "Names in Search of a Concept: Maturity, Fluency, Complexity, and Growth in Written Syntax," *College Composition and Communication* 31 (1980): 291–300.

———, John A. Daly, and Stephen P. Witte. "The Role of Writing Apprehension in Writing Performance and Competence," *Journal of Educational Research* 75 (Sept.–Oct. 1981): 16–21.

———, Thomas P. Miller, Paul R. Meyer, and Stephen P. Witte. *Writing after College: A Stratified Survey of the Writing of College-Trained People*, FIPSE Grant G008005896, Technical Report no. 1. Austin: Writing Program Assessment Office, Univ. of Texas, 1981. ERIC Doc. no. ED 210 708.

———, and Anna Skinner. *Writers' Processes and Writers' Knowledge: A Review of Research*, FIPSE Grant G008005896, Technical Report no. 6. Austin: Writing Program Assessment Office, Univ. of Texas, 1982.

———, and Stephen Witte. "Analyzing Revision," *College Composition and Communication* 32 (1981): 400–14.

Flanders, Ned A. "Interaction Analysis in the Classroom: A Manual for Observers." In *Mirrors for Behavior*, vol. 2, ed. by Anita Simon and E. Gil Boyer. Philadelphia: Research for Better Schools, 1967.

Flower, Linda, and John R. Hayes. "The Cognition of Discovery: Defining a Rhetorical Problem," *College Composition and Communication* 31 (1980): 21–32.

———. "A Cognitive Process Theory of Writing," *College Composition and Communication* 32 (1981): 365–87.

———. "The Pregnant Pause: An Inquiry into the Nature of Planning," *Research in the Teaching of English* 15 (1981): 229–44.

Frederiksen, Carl. "Abilities, Transfer and Information Retrieval in Verbal Learning," *Multivariate Behavior Research Monographs* 2 (1969): 1–82.

Freedman, Sarah W. "Evaluation in the Writing Conference: An Interactive Process." In *Selected Papers from the 1981 Texas Writing Research Conference*, ed. by Maxine Hairston and Cynthia Selfe, pp. 65–96. Austin: Univ. of Texas, 1981. ERIC Doc. no. ED 208 417.

————. "Influences on Evaluators of Expository Essays: Beyond the Test," *Research in the Teaching of English* 15 (1981): 245–55.

————, and Robert Calfee. "Holistic Assessment of Writing: Experimental Design and Cognitive Theory." Unpublished MS.

Fulwiler, Toby, and Art Young, eds. *Language Connections: Writing and Reading Across the Curriculum*. Urbana: National Council of Teachers of English, 1982.

Gage, N. L., ed. *Handbook of Research in Teaching*. Chicago: Rand McNally, 1963.

Gagne, Robert. *The Conditions of Learning*, 2d ed. New York: Holt, 1970.

Gardner, Don E. "Five Evaluation Frameworks: Implications for Decision Making in Higher Education," *Journal of Higher Education* 48 (1977): 571–93.

Garrison, Roger. "One to One: Tutorial Instruction in Freshman Composition." In *New Directions for Community Colleges*, pp. 55–83. San Francisco: Jossey-Bass, 1974.

Gaynor, Judith L. "A Comparison of Direct and Indirect Assessments of Writing Skills," *Journal of Educational Measurement* 16 (1979): 119–28.

Gebhardt, Richard. "Teamwork and Feedback: Broadening the Base of Collaborative Writing," *College English* 42 (1980): 69–74.

Gibson, Walker, ed. *New Students in Two-Year Colleges: Twelve Essays*. Urbana: National Council of Teachers of English, 1979.

Glass, G. V. *The Growth of Evaluation Methodology*. Boulder: Laboratory of Educational Research, Univ. of Colorado, 1969.

————, ed. *Evaluation Studies Review Annual*, vol. 1. Beverly Hills: Sage, 1976.

Glutthorn, Allan A. "Cooperate and Create: Teaching Writing Through Small Groups," *English Journal* 62 (Dec. 1973): 1274–75.

Godshalk, Fred, Frances Swineford, and William E. Coffman. *The Measurement of Writing Ability*. New York: College Entrance Examination Board, 1966.

Goldman, Roy D., and David J. Hudson. "A Multivariate Analysis of Academic Abilities and Strategies for Successful and Unsuccessful College

Students in Different Major Fields," *Journal of Educational Psychology* 65 (1973): 364–70.

————, and Rebecca Warren. "Discriminant Analysis of Study Strategies Connected with Grade Success in Different Major Fields," *Journal of Educational Measurement* 10 (1973): 39–47.

Goody, Jack. *Domestication of the Savage Mind.* Cambridge: Cambridge Univ. Pr., 1977.

————. *Literacy in Traditional Societies.* Cambridge: Cambridge Univ. Pr., 1969.

Gorrell, Robert M., ed. *Rhetoric: Theories for Application.* Champaign: National Council of Teachers of English, 1967.

Grady, Michael. "A Conceptual Rhetoric of the Composition," *College Composition and Communication* 22 (1971): 348–54.

Guba, Egon G., and Charles E. Bidwell. *Administrative Relationships: Teacher Effectiveness, Teacher Satisfaction and Administrative Behaviour.* Chicago: Univ. of Chicago, Midwest Administrative Centre, 1957.

Hairston, Maxine. "The Winds of Change: Thomas Kuhn and Revolution in the Teaching of Writing," *College Composition and Communication* 33 (1982): 76–88.

————, and Cynthia Selfe, eds. *Selected Papers from the 1981 Texas Writing Research Conference.* Austin: Univ. of Texas, 1981. ERIC Doc. no. ED 208 417.

Halliday, M. A. K. *Language as a Social Semiotic: The Social Interpretation of Meaning.* Baltimore: Univ. Park Pr., 1978.

Hammond, K. R., C. J. Hursh, and F. J. Todd. "Analyzing the Components of Clinical Inference," *Psychological Review* 72 (1965): 215–24.

Harris, Muriel. "Individualized Diagnosis: Teaching for Causes, Not Symptoms, of Writing Deficiencies," *College English* 40 (Nov. 1978): 318–23.

Harrow, Anita. *A Taxonomy of the Psychomotor Domain.* New York: David McKay, 1972.

Haswell, Richard H. "Tactics of Discourse: A Classification for Student Writers," *College English* 43 (Feb. 1981): 168–78.

Havinghurst, R. *Developmental Tasks and Education,* 3d ed. New York: David McKay, 1973.

Havelock, Eric A. *Origins of Western Literacy.* Toronto: Ontario Institute for Studies in Education, 1976.

Hawkins, Thom. *Group Inquiry Techniques for Teaching Writing.* Urbana, IL: National Council of Teachers of English and the ERIC Clearinghouse on Reading and Communication Skills, 1976.

———. "Intimacy and Audience: The Relationship Between Revision and the Social Dimension of Peer Tutoring," *College English* 42 (1980): 64–68.

Heath, Shirley Brice. "The Functions and Uses of Literacy," *Journal of Communication* 30 (1980): 123–33.

———. "Toward an Ethnohistory of Writing in American Education." In *Writing: The Nature, Development, and Teaching of Written Communication; Volume 1, Variation in Writing: Functional and Linguistic-Cultural Differences*, ed. by Marcia Farr Whiteman, pp. 25–45. Hillsdale, NJ: Lawrence Erlbaum, 1981.

Hipple, Theodore W. "The Grader's Helpers—Colleagues, Peers, and Scorecards," *English Journal* 61 (May 1972): 690–93.

House, Ernest R. *Evaluating with Validity*. Beverly Hills and London: Sage, 1980.

———, ed. *School Evaluation*. Berkeley: McCutchan, 1973.

Hunt, Kellogg. "Early Blooming and Late Blooming Syntactic Structures." In *Evaluating Writing: Describing, Measuring, Judging*, ed. by Charles R. Cooper and Lee Odell, pp. 91–104. Urbana: National Council of Teachers of English, 1977.

Jewell, Ross M., John Cowley, and Gordon Rhum. *The Effectiveness of College-Level Instruction in Freshman Composition*, Final Report, Project no. 2188. Washington, DC: Office of Education, U.S. Department of Health, Education, and Welfare, 1969.

———. *Interim Report: The Effectiveness of College-Level Instruction in Freshman Composition*, Cooperative Research Project no. 2188. Cedar Falls: State College of Iowa, 1966.

Johnson, Lois V. "Children's Writing in Three Forms of Composition," *Elementary English* 44 (1967): 265–69.

Joyce, Bruce R. "A Problem of Categories: Classifying Approaches to Teaching," *Journal of Education* 160 (Aug. 1978): 67–95.

———, and M. Weil. *Models of Teaching*. Englewood Cliffs: Prentice-Hall, 1979.

Judy, Stephen. "The Experiential Approach: Inner Worlds to Outer Worlds." In *Eight Approaches to Teaching Composition*, ed. by Timothy R. Donovan and Ben W. McClelland, pp. 37–51. Urbana: National Council of Teachers of English, 1981.

Kaplan, A., A. L. Skogstad, and M. A. Girshick. "The Prediction of Social and Technological Events," *Public Opinion Quarterly* 14 (1950): 93–110.

Kasden, Lawrence N., and Daniel R. Hoeber, eds. *Basic Writing: Essays for Teachers, Researchers, and Administrators.* Urbana: National Council of Teachers of English, 1980.

Kemmis, Stephen. "Telling It Like It Is: The Problem of Making a Portrayal of an Education Program." In *Curriculum Handbook: Administration and Theory,* vol. 2, ed. by Louis Rubin, pp. 359–71. Boston: Allyn & Bacon, 1977.

Kerek, Andrew. "The Combining Process." In *Selected Papers from the 1981 Texas Writing Research Conference,* ed. by Maxine Hairston and Cynthia Selfe, pp. 97–115. Austin: Univ. of Texas, 1981. ERIC Doc. no. ED 208 417.

———, Donald Daiker, and Max Morenberg. "Sentence Combining and College Composition," *Perceptual and Motor Skills* 51 (1980): 1059–1167 (Monograph Supplement 1-V51).

Kinghorn, Norton, Lester Faigley, and Thomas Clemens. *A Syntactic Approach to College Writing: An Analysis of Theory and Effect.* Grand Forks: Univ. of North Dakota Study Group on Evaluation, 1981.

Kinneavy, James L. "The Basic Aims of Discourse," *College Composition and Communication* 20 (1969): 297–313.

———. "Sentence Combining in a Comprehensive Language Framework." In *Sentence Combining and the Teaching of Writing,* ed. by Donald Daiker, Andrew Kerek, and Max Morenberg, pp. 60–76. Akron: L & S Books, 1979.

———. "Theories of Composition and Actual Writing," *Kansas English* 58 (Dec. 1973): 3–17.

———. *A Theory of Discourse.* 1971. Reprint. New York: Norton, 1980.

———. "Translating Theory into Practice in Teaching Composition: A Historical and a Contemporary View." In *Classical Rhetoric in Modern Discourse,* ed. by Robert J. Conners, Lisa Ede, and Andrea Lunsford. Carbondale: Southern Illinois Univ. Pr., *in press.*

———, John Q. Cope, and J. W. Campbell. *Aims and Audiences.* Dubuque: Kendall/Hunt, 1976.

———. *Writing—Basic Modes of Organization.* Dubuque: Kendall/Hunt, 1976.

Kitzhaber, Albert R. *Themes, Theories, and Therapy: The Teaching of College Writing.* New York: McGraw-Hill, 1963.

Klaus, Carl H. *Style in English Prose.* New York: Macmillan, 1969.

Krathwohl, David R., Benjamin S. Bloom, and Bertram B. Masia. *Taxonomy of Educational Objectives, Handbook II: Affective Domain.* New York: David McKay, 1956.

Kroll, Barry. "Developmental Perspectives and the Teaching of Composition," *College English* 41 (1980): 741–52.

Larkin, Ralph W. "Contextual Influences on Teacher Leadership Styles," *Sociology of Education* 46 (1973): 471–79.

Larson, Richard L., and the CCCC Committee on Teaching and Its Evaluation in Composition. "Evaluating Instruction in Writing: Approaches and Instruments," *College Composition and Communication* 33 (May 1982): 213–29.

Levin, Gerald, ed. *Prose Models*. New York: Harcourt, 1975.

Lewy, Arieh, ed. *Handbook of Curriculum Evaluation*. Paris and New York: UNESCO and Longman, 1977.

Liede, Goran. "Experts Judgments as Evaluation Data." In *Handbook of Curriculum Evaluation*, ed. by Arieh Lewy, pp. 167–88. Paris and New York: UNESCO and Longman, 1977.

Linquist, E. F., ed. *Educational Measurement*. Washington, DC: American Council on Education, 1951.

Lipsitz, Lawrence, ed. *The Test Score Decline: Meaning and Issues*. Englewood Cliffs: Educational Technology Publications, 1977.

Lunsford, Andrea A. "Cognitive Development and the Basic Writer," *College English* 41 (Sept. 1979): 39–46.

McCrimmon, James. *Writing with a Purpose*, 6th ed. Boston: Houghton, 1976.

McPherson, Elizabeth. "Composition." In *The Teaching of English, the 76th Yearbook of the National Society for the Study of Education*, pt. 1, ed. by James R. Squire, pp. 178–88. Chicago: National Society for the Study of Education, 1977.

Macklin, John H. *Classical Rhetoric for Modern Discourse: An Art of Invention, Arrangement, and Style for Readers, Speakers, and Writers*. New York: Free Pr., 1969.

Macrorie, Ken. *Telling Writing*. Rochelle Park, NJ: Hayden, 1970.

———. *Writing to Be Read*. Rochelle Park, NJ: Hayden, 1968.

Mann, John. "The Outcome of Evaluation Research." In *Evaluating Action Programs: Readings in Social Action and Education*. Boston: Allyn & Bacon, 1972.

Mellon, John C. "Issues in the Theory and Practice of Sentence Combining: A Twenty-Year History." In *Sentence Combining and the Teaching of Writing*, ed. by Donald Daiker, Andrew Kerek, and Max Morenberg, pp. 1–38. Akron: L & S Books, 1979.

———. *National Assessment and the Teaching of English.* Urbana; National Council of Teachers of English, 1975.

———. "Round Two of the National Assessment—Interpreting the Apparent Decline in Writing Ability: A Review," *Research in the Teaching of English* 10 (1976): 66–74.

———. *Transformational Sentence Combining: A Method for Enhancing Syntactic Fluency in English Composition,* Research Report no. 10. Champaign: National Council of Teachers of English, 1969.

Millman, Jason, ed. *Handbook of Teacher Evaluation.* Beverly Hills: Sage, in cooperation with the National Council on Educational Measurement, 1981.

Moffett, James. "Evaluation of the Writing Programs at the University of California San Diego." In Donald Wesling et al., *Evaluation of the Four College Writing Programs at UC San Diego.* San Diego: Univ. of California, 1978.

———. "A Rationale for a New Curriculum in English." In *Rhetoric: Theories for Application,* ed. by Robert M. Gorrell, pp. 114–21. Champaign: National Council of Teachers of English, 1967.

———. "A Structural Curriculum in English," *Harvard Educational Review* 36 (1966): 17–28.

———. *Teaching the Universe of Discourse.* Boston: Houghton, 1968.

Morenberg, Max, Donald Daiker, and Andrew Kerek. "Sentence Combining at the College Level: An Experimental Study," *Research in the Teaching of English* 12 (1978): 245–56.

Morris, Norman. "An Historian's View of Examinations." In *Examinations and English Education,* ed. by Stephen Wiseman, pp. 1–43. Manchester: Manchester Univ. Pr., 1961.

Murray, Donald M. *A Writer Teaches Writing: A Practical Method of Teaching Composition.* Boston: Houghton, 1968.

National Assessment of Educational Progress. *Writing Achievement, 1969–79: Results from the Third National Writing Assessment, Volume I—17-Year-Olds,* Report no. 10-W-01. Denver: National Assessment of Educational Progress, 1980.

———. *Writing Achievement, 1969–79: Results from the Third National Assessment, Volume II—13-Year-Olds,* Report no. 10-W-02. Denver: National Assessment of Educational Progress, 1980.

———. *Writing Achievement, 1969–79: Results from the Third National Assessment, Volume III—9-Year-Olds,* Report no. 10-W-03. Denver: National Assessment of Educational Progress, 1980.

Nold, Ellen W., and Sarah W. Freedman. "An Analysis of Readers' Responses to Essays," *Research in the Teaching of English* 11 (1977): 164–74.

Nugent, Harold E. "The Role of Old and New Information in Sentence Combining." In *Sentence Combining and the Teaching of Writing*, ed. by Donald Daiker, Andrew Kerek, and Max Morenberg, pp. 201–8. Akron: L & S Books, 1979.

Odell, Lee. "Defining and Assessing Competence in Writing." In *The Nature and Measurement of Competence in English*, ed. by Charles R. Cooper, pp. 95–138. Urbana, IL: National Council of Teachers of English, 1981.

———. "Teachers of Composition and Needed Research in Discourse Theory," *College Composition and Communication* 30 (1979): 39–45.

———, and Charles R. Cooper. "Procedures for Evaluating Writing: Assumptions and Needed Research," *College English* 42 (1980): 35–43.

O'Hare, Frank. *Sentence Combining: Improving Student Writing Without Formal Grammar Instruction*, Research Report no. 15. Champaign: National Council of Teachers of English, 1973.

Ohmann, Richard. *English in America*. New York: Oxford Univ. Pr., 1976.

Olson, Paul. *A View of Power: Four Essays on the National Assessment of Educational Progress*. Grand Forks: Univ. of North Dakota Study Group on Evaluation, 1976.

Palacas, Arthur L. "Towards Teaching the Logic of Sentence Connection." In *Sentence Combining and the Teaching of Writing*, ed. by Donald Daiker, Andrew Kerek, and Max Morenberg, pp. 192–200. Akron: L & S Books, 1979.

Patton, Michael Quinn. *Qualitative Evaluation Methods*. Beverly Hills and London: Sage, 1980.

———. *Utilization-Focused Evaluation*. Beverly Hills: Sage, 1978.

Peters, Lawrence. "Writing Across the Curriculum: Across the U.S." Unpublished paper, George Mason Univ., 1982.

Peterson, P. L., and H. J. Walberg, eds. *Research on Teaching*. Berkeley: McCutchan, 1979.

Piaget, Jean. *Judgment and Reasoning in the Child*. London: Kegan Paul, 1928.

———. *The Language and Thought of the Child*. New York: New American Library, 1978.

———. *Six Psychological Studies*. New York: Random, 1967.

Popham, W. James. *Educational Evaluation*. Englewood Cliffs: Prentice-Hall, 1975.

Postlethwaite, T. Neville. "Determination of General Educational Aims and Objectives." In *Handbook of Curriculum Evaluation*, ed. by Arieh Lewy, pp. 37–61. New York: UNESCO and Longman, 1977.

Rasp, A. F. "Delphi: A Strategy for Decision Implementation," *Educational Planning* 1 (1974): 42–47.

Raygor, A. L. *McGraw-Hill Basic Skills System Reading Test: Examiner's Manual*. New York: McGraw-Hill, 1970.

———. *McGraw-Hill Basic Skills System Writing Test: Examiner's Manual*. New York: McGraw-Hill, 1970.

Rice, Warner. "A Proposal for the Abolition of Freshman English, As It Is Now Commonly Taught, from the College Curriculum," *College English* 21 (Apr. 1960): 361–67.

Rohman, D. Gordon. "Pre-Writing: The Stage of Discovery in the Writing Process," *College Composition and Communication* 16 (1965): 106–12.

———, and Albert O. Wlecke. *Pre-Writing: The Construction and Application of Models for Concept Formation in Writing*. U.S. Office of Education Cooperative Research Project no. 2174. East Lansing: Michigan State Univ., 1964.

Rose, Mike. "Sophisticated, Ineffective Books—The Dismantling of Process in Composition Texts," *College Composition and Communication* 32 (1981): 65–74.

Rossi, Peter H., and Sonia R. Wright. "Evaluation Research: An Assessment of Theory, Practice, and Politics," *Evaluation Quarterly* 1 (1977): 5–52.

Rubin, Louis, ed. *Curriculum Handbook: Administration and Theory*, vol. 2. Boston: Allyn & Bacon, 1977.

Rutman, Leonard. *Evaluation Research Methods: A Basic Guide*. Beverly Hills and London: Sage, 1977.

———. *Planning Useful Evaluations: Evaluability Assessment*. Berkeley and London: Sage, 1980.

Ryle, Gilbert. *The Concept of Mind*. New York: Barnes, 1949.

Schools Council. *Schools Council Working Paper Number Three*. London: Her Majesty's Stationery Office, 1965.

Scott, W. A. "Reliability of Content Analysis: The Case of Nominal Scale Coding," *Public Opinion Quarterly* 19 (1955): 321–25.

Scriven, Michael. "Evaluation Bias and Its Control." In *Evaluation Studies Review Annual*, vol. 1, ed. by G. V. Glass. Beverly Hills: Sage, 1976.

―――. "Goal Free Evaluation." In *School Evaluation*, ed. by Ernest R. House. Berkeley: McCutchan, 1973.

―――. "The Methodology of Evaluation." In *Perspectives on Curriculum Evaluation*, ed. by Ralph W. Tyler, pp. 39–83. Chicago: Rand McNally, 1967.

―――. "The Pros and Cons about Goal Free Evaluation," *Education Comment* 3 (1972): 1–4.

Seegars, J. C. "The Form of Discourse and Sentence Structure," *Elementary English* 10 (1933): 51–54.

Shaughnessy, Mina. "Basic Writing." In *Teaching Composition: 10 Bibliographical Essays*, ed. by Gary Tate, pp. 137–67. Fort Worth: Texas Christian Univ. Pr., 1976.

―――. "Diving In: An Introduction to Basic Writing," *College Composition and Communication* 27 (1976): 234–39.

―――. *Errors and Expectations: A Guide for the Teacher of Basic Writing.* New York: Oxford Univ. Pr., 1977.

Shulman, Lee S. "Disciplines of Inquiry in Education: An Overview," *Educational Researcher* 10 (June/July, 1981): 5–12, 23.

Shuy, Roger W. "A Holistic View of Language," *Research in the Teaching of English* 15 (1981): 101–11.

Simon, A., and E. G. Boyer, eds. *Mirrors for Behavior.* Philadelphia: Research for Better Schools, 1967.

Slovic, P. "Analyzing the Expert Judge: A Descriptive Study of a Stockbroker's Decision Processes," *Journal of Experimental Psychology* 78 (1968), monograph supplement, no. 3, pt. 2.

―――, and S. C. Lichtenstein. "Comparison of Bayesian and Regression Approaches to the Study of Information Processing in Judgment," *Organizational Behavior and Human Performance* 6 (1971): 649–744.

Smith, David L., and Barry J. Fraser. "Towards a Confluence of Quantitative and Qualitative Approaches to Curriculum Evaluation," *Journal of Curriculum Studies* 12 (1980): 367–70.

Sommers, Nancy I. "The Need for Theory in Composition Research," *College Composition and Communication* 31 (1979): 46–49.

―――. "Revision Strategies of Student Writers and Experienced Adult Writers," *College Composition and Communication* 31 (1980): 378–88.

Stake, Robert E. "Language, Rationality and Assessment." In *Improving Educational Assessment*, ed. by W. H. Beatty, pp. 14–40. Washington, DC: Association for Supervision and Curriculum Development, 1969.

———, ed. *Curriculum Evaluation*. Chicago: Rand McNally, 1967.

———. *Evaluating Educational Programmes: The Need and the Response*. Washington, DC: OECD Publications Center, 1976.

Stewart, Donald C. "Composition Textbooks and the Assault on Tradition," *College Composition and Communication* 29 (1978): 171–76.

Strong, William. *Sentence Combining: A Composing Book*. New York: Random, 1973.

Stufflebeam, Daniel I., W. J. Foley, W. J. Gephart, E. G. Guba, H. D. Hammond, and M. M. Provus. *Educational Evaluation and Decision-Making*. Itasca, IL: Peacock, 1971.

Suchman, Edward. *Evaluative Research*. New York: Russell Sage Foundation, 1967.

Squire, James R., ed. *The Teaching of English, the 76th Yearbook of the National Society for the Study of Education*, pt. 1. Chicago: National Society for the Study of Education, 1977.

Tate, Gary, ed. *Teaching Composition: 10 Bibliographical Essays*. Fort Worth: Texas Christian Univ. Pr., 1976.

Tyler, Ralph W. *Basic Principles of Curriculum and Instruction*. Chicago: Univ. of Chicago Pr., 1950.

———. "The Functions of Measurement in Improving Instruction." In *Educational Measurement*, ed. by E. F. Linquist, pp. 47–67. Washington, DC: American Council on Education, 1951.

———, ed. *Perspectives on Curriculum Evaluation*. Chicago: Rand McNally, 1967.

van Ek, J. A., with contributions by L. G. Alexander. *The Threshold Level for Modern Language Learning in Schools*. London: Longman, 1976.

Veal, L. Ramon, and Murray Tillman. "Mode of Discourse Variation in the Evaluation of Children's Writing," *Research in the Teaching of English* 5 (1971): 37–45.

Vygotsky, Lev Semenovich. *Language and Thought*, ed. and trans. by Eugenia Haufmann and Gertrude Vakar. Cambridge, MA: M.I.T. Pr., 1962.

Weinberg, A. M. *Reflections on Big Science*. Cambridge, MA: M.I.T. Pr., 1967.

Wesling, Donald, John Conlisk, Sharon Evans, W. G. Hardison, Ralph

Loveberg, Emory Tolberg, and Jane Watkins. *Evaluation of the Four College Writing Programs at UC San Diego.* San Diego: Univ. of California, 1978.

Whiteman, Marcia Farr, ed. *Writing: The Nature, Development, and Teaching of Written Communication; Volume 1, Variation in Writing: Functional and Linguistic-Cultural Differences.* Hillsdale, NJ: Lawrence Erlbaum, 1981.

Wiener, Harvey S. "Basic Writing: First Day's Thoughts on Process and Detail." In *Eight Approaches to Teaching Composition,* ed. by Timothy R. Donovan and Ben W. McClelland, pp. 87–99. Urbana: National Council of Teachers of English, 1981.

———. "Media Composition: Preludes to Writing," *College English* 35 (1974): 566–74.

Williams, Joseph M. "Defining Complexity," *College English* 40 (Jan. 1980): 595–609.

Winer, B. J. *Statistical Principles in Experimental Design,* 2d ed. New York: McGraw-Hill, 1971.

Wiseman, Stephen, ed. *Examinations and English Education.* Manchester: Manchester Univ. Pr., 1961.

Withal, John, W. W. Lewis, and John M. Newell. "Classroom Communication Observational Categories." In *Mirrors for Behavior,* vol. 13, ed. by Anita Simon and E. Gil Boyer. Philadelphia: Research for Better Schools, 1967.

Witte, Stephen P. "Review of *Sentence Combining and the Teaching of Writing,*" *College Composition and Communication* 31 (1980): 433–37.

———, Roger D. Cherry, and Paul R. Meyer. *The Goals of Freshman Writing Programs as Perceived by a National Sample of College and University Writing Program Directors and Teachers,* FIPSE Grant G008005896, Technical Report no. 5. Austin: Writing Program Assessment Office, Univ. of Texas, 1982. ERIC Doc. no. ED 216 395.

———, and Lester Faigley. *A Comparison of Analytic and Synthetic Approaches to the Teaching of College Writing,* TWRG Research Report no. 1. Austin: Department of English, Univ. of Texas, 1981. ERIC Doc. no. ED 209 677.

———, and Paul R. Meyer with Thomas P. Miller. *A National Survey of College and University Teachers of Writing,* FIPSE Grant G008005896, Technical Report no. 4. Austin: Writing Program Assessment Office, Univ. of Texas, 1982. ERIC Doc. no. ED 219 779.

———, and Lester Faigley. *A National Survey of College and University*

Writing Program Directors, FIPSE Grant G008005896 Technical Report no. 2. Austin: Writing Program Assessment Office, Univ. of Texas, 1981. ERIC Doc. no. ED 210 709.

Wittig, Susan. *Dialogue.* Iowa City: Conduit, 1978.

————. "Dialogue: Project C-BE Drill and Practice," *Pipeline* 4 (1978): 20–22.

————. *Steps to Structure.* Cambridge, MA: Winthrop, 1975.

Wolfe, Don M. *Creative Ways to Teach English.* New York: Odyssey, 1966.

Womer, F. B. *What Is National Assessment?* Ann Arbor: National Assessment of Educational Progress, 1970.

Woods, William F. "Composition Textbooks and Pedagogical Theory: A Review-Essay," *College English* 43 (1981): 393–409.

Worthen, Blaine R., and James R. Sanders, eds. *Educational Evaluation: Theory and Practice.* Worthington, OH: Charles A. Jones, 1973.

Writing Program Administrators Board of Consultant Evaluators. "Writing Program Evaluation: An Outline for Self-Study," *Journal of the Council of Writing Program Administrators* 4 (Winter 1980): 23–28.

Young, Richard E. "Paradigms and Problems: Needed Research in Rhetorical Invention." In *Research on Composing: Points of Departure,* ed. by Charles R. Cooper and Lee Odell, pp. 29–47. Urbana: National Council of Teachers of English, 1978.

Yow, Chew Tow. "Evaluation at the Planning Stage." In *Handbook for Curriculum Evaluation,* ed. by Arieh Lewy, pp. 62–83. Paris and New York: UNESCO and Longman, 1977.

Zoellner, Robert. "Talk-Write: A Behavioral Pedagogy for Composition," *College English* 30 (1969): 267–320.

————. "On Zoellnerism," *College English* 30 (1969): 645–68.